The Mongols: A Very Short Introduction

VERY SHORT INTRODUCTIONS are for anyone wanting a stimulating and accessible way in to a new subject. They are written by experts and have been published in more than 25 languages worldwide.

The series began in 1995 and now represents a wide variety of topics in history, philosophy, religion, science, and the humanities. The VSI library now contains more than 300 volumes—a Very Short Introduction to everything from ancient Egypt and Indian philosophy to conceptual art and cosmology—and will continue to grow in a variety of disciplines.

Available soon:

For more information visit our website

www.oup.co.uk/general/vsi/

Morris Rossabi

THE MONGOLS

A Very Short Introduction

OXFORD
UNIVERSITY PRESS

OXFORD

UNIVERSITY PRESS

Oxford University Press, Inc., publishes works that further
Oxford University's objective of excellence
in research, scholarship, and education.

Oxford   New York
Auckland   Cape Town   Dar es Salaam   Hong Kong   Karachi
Kuala Lumpur   Madrid   Melbourne   Mexico City   Nairobi
New Delhi   Shanghai   Taipei   Toronto

With offices in
Argentina   Austria   Brazil   Chile   Czech Republic   France   Greece
Guatemala   Hungary   Italy   Japan   Poland   Portugal   Singapore
South Korea   Switzerland   Thailand   Turkey   Ukraine   Vietnam

Published by Oxford University Press, Inc.
198 Madison Avenue, New York, NY 10016

www.oup.com

Oxford is a registered trademark of Oxford University Press

Library of Congress Cataloging-in-Publication Data
Rossabi, Morris.
The Mongols : a very short introduction / Morris Rossabi.
p.   cm.
Includes bibliographical references and index.
ISBN 978-0-19-984089-2 (pbk)
1. Mongols—History. I. Title.
DS19.R67   2012
950'.2—dc23   2011041803

Printed and bound by
CPI Group (UK) Ltd, Croydon, CR0 4YY

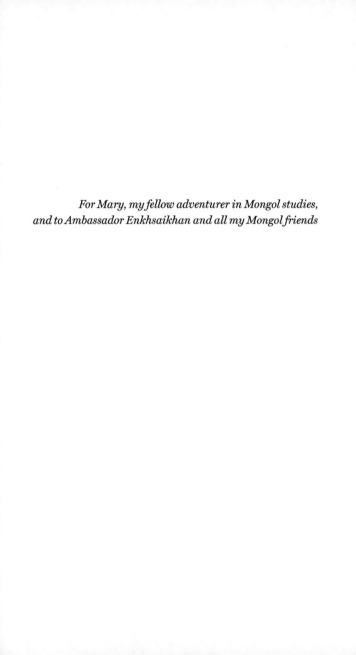

For Mary, my fellow adventurer in Mongol studies,
and to Ambassador Enkhsaikhan and all my Mongol friends

Contents

List of illustrations and maps

Acknowledgments

As a young researcher, I had the good fortune to meet and converse with a fine group of scholars of Chinese and Mongol studies. After four decades of research, this book is a synthesis of my current understanding of the Mongol empire, and I wish to acknowledge a few of the scholars who influenced my thinking. They ought not to be blamed for any faulty interpretations in this work, and indeed probably some would surely have disagreed with my views. Many of those I will mention are gone, but they have left a lasting impression on me.

Professor Joseph Fletcher Jr., of Harvard University, was my closest friend and colleague in the field. Although our scholarly interests did not necessarily coincide, we often discussed our research, which deepened our understanding of Inner Asian history. He devoted considerable effort and time to mastering a slew of foreign languages, including Russian, Chinese, Japanese, Manchu, Mongolian, Arabic, French, German, Spanish, and Persian. Succumbing to a virulent form of cancer in 1984, he did not write the important works for which he had prepared so assiduously. Yet his teaching and encouragement of younger scholars had a significant impact on the field of Mongol studies.

Owen Lattimore and Professor Denis Sinor, of Indiana University, were pioneers in the field and deserve immense credit for bringing

Mongolia to the attention of educated readers. Although I did not know Lattimore well, in our few meetings from 1969 on, I recognized that he held a fountain of ideas about the Mongol empire. I knew Denis Sinor quite well, and his enthusiasm for Mongol studies was infectious. He commissioned me to write several articles early in my career and generously provided careful evaluation of these papers.

A number of people trained me in Chinese history and in writing. Professor L. Carrington Goodrich, of Columbia University, employed me at the Ming Biographical History Project to write about prominent Central Asians and Mongols of the Ming era. A wonderful gentleman, he taught me to be more careful and precise in my writing and thinking. Professor Hans Bielenstein, also of Columbia, insisted (and still insists) on accurate translations of Classical Chinese texts, an emphasis that has been helpful throughout my career. Sheila Levine, of the University of California Press, taught me much about writing for a general educated reader.

Others to whom I owe much include the late Professor John Langlois, formerly of Bowdoin College, the late Sherman Lee, formerly director of the Cleveland Museum of Art , and the late John Pope, formerly director of the Freer Gallery of Art. I have also benefited from friendships with Professor Leonard Blusse of Leiden University, Dr. Stan Czuma, retired curator of South Asian Art at the Cleveland Museum of Art, Jargalsaikhan Enkhsaikhan, ambassador of Mongolia to Austria, the late Professor Herbert Franke of the University of Munich, Professor Michael Gasster of Rutgers University, Professor Ralph Kauz of Bonn University, Dr. Yuki Konagaya of the National Museum of Ethnology in Osaka, Professor David Morgan of the University of Wisconsin, Professor Roderich Ptak of the University of Munich, Professor Carl Riskin of Queens College and Columbia University, Professor Jonathan Spence of Yale University, and Professor John Wills of the University of Southern California.

The book has been improved through Nancy Toff's careful editing and Sonia Tycko's technical expertise concerning maps and other illustrations. Ms. Toff's queries about unclear passages and obtuse phrasing in the original text have prompted revisions that have, I hope, resulted in a clearer narrative. I am truly grateful for her assistance.

On a personal level, I would like to thank the undergraduate and graduate students in my courses on Mongol History at Queens College and Columbia University for asking penetrating questions and demanding clear responses. Most significant, I have learned a great deal from my wife, Mary, in our collaboration on three books. I thank her for this and for much else. Others who have facilitated my work include Amy Rossabi, Tony Rossabi, Howard Sterinbach, Sarah and Nathan Sterinbach, Anna Zhivotovsky, and Julia Rossabi. I am grateful to them all.

A note on Romanization and pronunciation

For the convenience of the general reader, I have eliminated diacritical marks except for the umlaut, which has become fairly standard in English-language works. I have used the pinyin system of Romanization for all Chinese terms and names, and I have adopted Antoine Mostaert's scheme for the transliteration of Mongolian, as modified by Francis W. Cleaves, except for these deviations:

č is ch
š is sh
γ is gh
q is kh
ĵ is j

I have used a standard system of transcription, but without diacritical marks, for the very few Iranian names (e.g., Rashid al-Din).

A guide to pronunciation of pinyin for speakers of English includes the following:

q: an aspirated *ch* as in chin
zh: *j* as in jar
c: *ts* as in its
x: *sh* as in shore
z: *ds* as in moods

ai: sounds like eye
ao: *ow* as in how
ia: *yah*
ian: *yen*
ie: *yeah*
io: *yo*
i: *ee* as in see
i: (after c, ch, s, sh, zh, z): *er* as in her
e: *uh*
ei: *ai* as in stay
en: *en* as in happen
eng: *ung* as in sung
ong: *oong*
ou: *o* as in toe

A guide to pronunciation of Mongolian for speakers of English includes the following:

gh: a guttural hard *g*
kh: a guttural *ch* as in Loch Ness

Genealogical chart of prominent Mongol khans

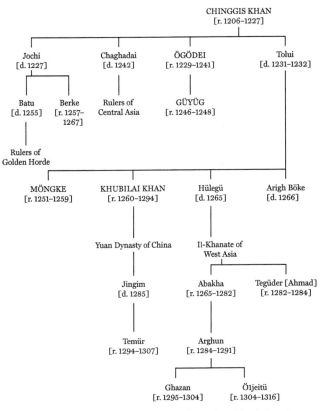

*Names in capital letters denote Khaghans or Great Khans, rulers of the whole empire.

Chapter 1
Life on the steppes

Two contemporary observations of the Mongols at their height in the thirteenth century convey divergent views. The Iranian historian Juvaini describes how the Mongol unifier Chinggis Khan (more commonly known in the West as Genghis Khan) attacked the Central Asian cities of Bukhara, a center of Islamic learning, and Samarkand, a great emporium and a vital halting place along the Silk Roads that traversed Eurasia. Mongol troops surrounded the towns and unleashed a barrage of arrows, fire arrows and fire lances, pots of naphtha (or perhaps incendiary bombs), and huge boulders and arrows hurled from catapults. Fires engulfed the cities, prompting the defenders to surrender. Mongol soldiers then torched the mostly wooden buildings in Bukhara. Thirty thousand people in Bukhara, who were taller than the butt of a whip, were killed. Mongol troops in Samarkand then destroyed the principal mosque, killed many inhabitants, raped numerous women, and virtually enslaved the remaining women and children, although Chinggis Khan ordered them to spare the lives of thirty thousand craftsmen.

This savagery and allegedly animal-like behavior was reinforced by the Mongols' lifestyle. Their dependence on animals for food, clothing, shelter, fuel, and medicines contributed to this image. Foreigners also noticed their seemingly special relationship with their horses. Their identification with their animals, which were essential for their very survival, and their aversion to washing their clothes, due to unwillingness to waste water and a traditional fear that washing would prompt Heaven to unleash thunderstorms on their settlements, were perceived as evidence of their barbarism.

On the other hand, the Venetian traveler Marco Polo writes about the concern of Chinggis Khan's grandson Khubilai Khan for the welfare of the Chinese people whom he had subjugated, a concern that the Chinese dynastic history also documented. Khubilai sent agents in summer throughout China to assess conditions in the countryside. If they found peasants whose land had been ravaged by storms, wind, or locusts and other pests, Khubilai would grant them grain from his storehouses and would relieve them of their tax burdens. Similarly, he dispatched officials in winter to determine whether herds had suffered or, in some cases, perished because of heavy snow or lightning or insufficient fodder. Marco Polo also portrays Khubilai as a sage and often benevolent ruler who appreciated beauty and supported the building of such well-planned cities as Daidu (modern Beijing) and Shangdu (Samuel Taylor Coleridge's "Xanadu"), and patronized the native arts and crafts. Naturally, he also depicts Khubilai's brutal suppression of rebel leaders and his destructive campaigns against South China, Japan, and Southeast Asia, but he generally offers a positive image of the Mongol emperor.

The Mongols' conquests and the governments they established initiated the first stirrings of contacts between Europe and East Asia, via the Silk Roads that had traditionally facilitated trade between China and the Middle East, and generated economic and cultural advances in the civilizations they ruled. To be sure, the subjugated populations themselves often developed the economic institutions, the technological innovations, and the literary, religious, and artistic texts and works that characterized their civilizations during the era of Mongol governance. Yet Mongol rule and the stability they brought paved the way for such remarkable developments. They also contributed by facilitating travel and trade along the Silk Roads, prompting interactions among far-flung civilizations. Splendid Iranian histories, beautiful Chinese textiles and porcelains, and exquisite Russian gold vessels were some of the products of such cultural interrelationships. Summer palaces at Takht-i Sulaiman (in Iran) and Shangdu (in Inner Mongolia) attested to the Mongols' patronage and grandiose aspirations.

How can these two differing and contradictory images of the Mongols be reconciled? Were they bloodthirsty murderers, rapists, and destroyers who simply sought booty from civilizations they conquered? Were they avengers of the Mongol Sky God Tenggeri, who allegedly entrusted them with the mission of conquering the world? Were they getting even with states that had denied them trade for essential goods? Or, after the initial invasions, did they seek to stabilize the areas they ruled? Did they contribute to peace by unifying such countries as China, which had suffered from having been broken up for centuries? Did the unity the Mongols imposed on much of Asia have salutary effects on culture?

The records on the Mongol Empire frequently impede attempts to answer these questions. Because the only Mongol primary source is *The Secret History of the Mongols*, a semi-mythical and semi-accurate work, nearly all accounts of their outburst on the world were written by those whom they had subjugated. *The Secret History* principally records Chinggis's rise to power, and it ends before the most important far-flung campaigns and invasions. Armenian, Syriac, Latin, Russian, and other foreign sources often portray the Mongols as murderous marauders who undermined development in regions they subjugated.

Massacres and devastation of regions were part of but not the whole Mongol story. Recent developments in the archaeology of various areas of the Mongol Empire, studies of artifacts produced or commissioned by the Mongols, and a careful re-reading and evaluation of foreign sources have provided alternative narratives. Russian archaeologists in the 1930s and 1940s and German researchers over the past decade have dug in the ruins of the ancient Mongol capital of Khara Khorum, and Japanese archaeologists in the 1930s and Chinese specialists during the past twenty years have excavated Shangdu, Khubilai Khan's summer capital. They have found exquisite Buddhist statues, jade belt ornaments, gold bracelets, temple frescos, and blue-and-white porcelains, confirming the sophisticated tastes of the Mongol rulers. Similar excavations of the Mongol summer capital of Takht-i Sulaiman in Iran and of many Mongol sites in Russia have uncovered beautiful tiles, Chinese porcelains, silk fabrics, and gold belts and goblets, offering a different and less negative perspective on Mongol appreciation of culture.

Similarly, the Chinese and Korean dynastic histories, as well as histories written by individual Chinese, offer a more nuanced appraisal of Mongol rule. Juvaini and Rashid al-Din, the great Iranian historians who served as officials at the Mongol court in the city of Tabriz, present a balanced evaluation of Mongol influence in the Middle East. Franciscan missionaries and, especially, Marco Polo, who wrote accounts of their travels and stays in Mongolia and China, were impressed by the Mongol rulers and their administration of China and provide readers with more positive views.

Land of the Blue Sky

The Mongols' traditional territories are landlocked and far enough from the ocean to block its moderating influence. The resulting extreme continental climate, with its cold temperatures and strong winds, pose severe challenges to human habitation. Long winters, with below-freezing temperatures from November through March and freezing temperatures in October and April, an elevation considerably above sea level, a short growing season, and brief summers, with unreliable and often relatively limited precipitation, preclude agriculture, except in specific circumscribed areas. About 1 percent of the land is arable, 8–10 percent is forested, and the rest is pasture land or desert. Half the

land is subject to permafrost, and the lakes and rivers freeze over
in winter, still another impediment to agriculture and human life.
The Gobi, which covers most of southern Mongolia, is classified
as a desert steppe region, but its heat and aridity have meant that
only the camel, of the five animals that the Mongols have relied
on, can comfortably survive in this environment. A few herders
have raised sheep and goats in this difficult terrain, but most have
eked out a living in the pasture lands north and west of the Gobi.
Even they faced perils in this fragile ecosystem. Winter blizzards
have plagued the country every few years and have created the
devastating and dreaded *zud*, or severe weather when the ground
is covered with snow and ice, preventing the animals from
reaching the life-saving grass and plants.

Only the hardiest of herders have survived under these conditions,
and the population in this vast domain is tiny, compared to that
of China, Mongolia's closest neighbor. The total population was
probably less than a million while China's population reached
seventy-five million during the Mongol invasions. Present-day
Mongolia, not to mention Inner Mongolia, Buryatia, and Tuva,
where the Mongols traditionally nomadized, is at least three
times the size of France. Thus distances between various groups
and confederations on the eve of the Mongol onslaughts of the
thirteenth century were often vast, and the Mongol peoples faced
almost insurmountable obstacles in attempting to achieve unity.
Despite these impediments, Mongolia had about 250 cloudless
days a year, more than almost any territory so far to the north, and
earned it the sobriquet of Land of the Blue Sky.

A key to survival in this vast terrain was mobility. Although
most groups moved principally from summer quarters to winter
encampments, they would sometimes migrate considerable
distances to avoid a *zud*. When *a zud* hit, they needed to move
their herds quickly, to far-flung locations to find sufficient
water and grass for their animals. Indeed, their lives centered
on the drive to feed and water their animals. In short, this

was a demanding lifestyle in one of the world's most perilous environments. Physical strength was essential, but skills and knowledge were also critical. A herder had to be familiar with the different plants each species required, to spot unusual animal behavior, to gauge the weather and its implications, to be aware of areas with lush vegetation, and to evaluate the sustainability of his quarters, not to mention knowledge of the market for his animals and animal products in order to obtain the optimal bartering arrangement for the products he needed.

Herders and their animals

Most important, herders needed to know about and have affection for their animals. The very first section of the *Secret History* bolsters the identification of Mongols with animals. It asserts that the union of a bluish wolf and a doe produced Chinggis Khan's ancestors and then proceeds to provide a lengthy genealogy, leading ultimately to Yisügei, Chinggis's father and a member of the Borjigin (or Gold) lineage.

The Mongols, as nomadic pastoralists, relied upon five principal animals. Sheep, both the most numerous and most valuable, provided food, clothing, and shelter. Mutton, which was often boiled and then carved with daggers at mealtime, was integral to the Mongol diet; the pastoralists obtained wool and animal skins to fashion their garments, collected sheep dung for fuel, and pressed wool into felt, which was used both for clothing, rugs, and blankets, and for the *gers*, the tentlike structures in which the Mongols resided. Though less plentiful than sheep, goats were also vital. Mongols consumed goat meat, milk, and cheese, and the poor among them wore goat skins. Because goats were not as tough as sheep and needed more solicitous care, they could not survive in more demanding terrains. Their value was also diminished by their consumption to the very root of plants and grass, and thus their ensuing contribution to desertification. Yaks and oxen required excellent grazing grounds for survival and could not endure in desert or other marginal regions. They flourished only in the steppes or in the mountains and were less able to fend for themselves than sheep or goats. The Mongols not only ate yak meat and drank yak milk but also employed yaks and oxen to transport their belongings during their seasonal moves to new pasture areas.

The economic value of the remaining two animals, the camel and the horse, is at first glance less obvious, but both contributed to and influenced Mongol society. The Bactrian or two-humped camel permitted the Mongols to transport heavy loads through the desert and other inhospitable terrains because it could carry more weight than any other pack animal. It was ideally suited to lands in which water and grass were not always available. Camels could drink enormous quantities of water at a watering hole or lake and then continue for days without liquid. They required less pasture than other animals and could extract food from the scruffiest shrubs or blades of grass. Camels enabled the Mongols to carry goods for trade or to move their household belongings as they migrated to new pastures or to convey supplies or siege engines for their troops.

The horse had economic value but was also vital to the Mongols' military capabilities. Mongols ate horse meat and drank *airagh* (also known as *koumiss, comos,* or fermented mare's milk), and employed it in ceremonies and sacrifices. Horses offered them the mobility to let their animals loose to seek pasture during the day and to round up the herds in the evening. Perhaps even more important, war horses and their cavalry gave them a tactical advantage in conflicts with sedentary civilizations. While on campaign, their saddlebags contained cooking pots, dried meat, yoghurt, water bottles, and other essentials for lengthy expeditions. A wood-and-leather saddle, which was rubbed with sheep's fat to prevent cracking and shrinkage, allowed the horses to bear the weight of their riders and their equipment for long periods, and also permitted the riders to retain a firm seat. A sturdy stirrup enabled Mongol horsemen to be steadier and thus more accurate in shooting from horseback. Before combat, leather coverings were often placed on the head of each horse, and its body was frequently covered with armor.

Recognizing the value of their horses, Mongols were solicitous of their steeds. Each Mongol cavalryman normally had four or five horses, so that each horse he rode was, at one time or another, given a lengthy rest during a journey. Others carried equipment, while one or two had no load and were thus fresh for combat. The horses were small but strong and sturdy. The Mongols preferred geldings and mares, which were easier to manage than stallions, and mares had the advantage of producing milk. Horses also could, on rare occasions, provide sustenance to their riders on long trips during which all the food had been consumed. A rider would then cut the horse's veins and drink the blood that spurted forth. The Mongols' esteem for their horses was reflected in their burial practices. When a leading Mongol nobleman died, his horse was sacrificed and buried with him because he would need his trusted steed in the afterlife.

Despite their long associations with pastoralism, Mongols were originally not herders. Chinese sources indicate that the Mongols' ancestors inhabited the Siberian and Manchurian forests and survived by hunting and fishing. By the late tenth or early eleventh century, they moved to Mongolia, where they developed a nomadic pastoral society, but they maintained hunting as a subsidiary pursuit. Hunting provided them with additional food and sharpened their military skills. A few herders tilled the land in areas suitable for cultivation, supplementing their meager food resources. No matter how skillful the individual Mongol herder, a nomadic pastoral economy was precarious. The spread of disease among animals or a prolonged or hard winter or a summer drought could spell disaster. Most families had few reserves of food or other necessities because of their frequent migrations, which precluded accumulation of surplus resources. Constant travels also prevented the development of an artisan class. A craftsman found it difficult to move the sometimes numerous or bulky tools and machines that he required for his work. Thus the Mongols had few potters, weavers, and ironworkers; yet they needed pots, clothing, and simple iron tools.

The fragility of their economy and their need for products they themselves could not produce prompted the Mongols to seek commerce with China and Central Asia, their neighbors. They received craft articles and in return offered animals and animal products. In times of great distress, they sought and sometimes received grains or vegetables. They desperately needed products from the sedentary civilizations. If their neighbors denied them commerce, their only recourse was to raid to obtain the products they required. Initially, they traded for necessities, but as their leaders learned more about the sedentary civilizations, they began to crave such luxuries as silk.

Before the desire for extravagant and elegant foreign goods intruded, the Mongols lived modestly. Their food was simple, mostly meat and dairy products, and their clothing was fashioned for comfort and simplicity; they dressed either in tunics made of buckram and other coarse cloth or garments made of furs and generally wore leather boots with upturned toes. Their shelters known as *gers* were ideally suited to their lifestyles as they could easily be dismantled, moved by cart to another location, and then set up again. The *ger* had a round, domelike shape with a wall about ten feet high, on top of which was a roof, with an opening at its highest point. The wall consisted of a number of sticks laced together in a criss-cross pattern and then attached to the door frame. The opening at the roof permitted the smoke from the fireplace at the center of the *ger* to escape. A series of wooden poles supported the roof. Felt coverings were spread across the whole *ger* and tied down to the framework. Furs could then be added to the framework in winter, and both felt and furs could be removed in summer. Wooden beds with fur coverings, chests, and tables comprised the simple furnishings. Men traditionally occupied the left side of the *ger*, while women kept their belongings on the right side.

Groups and confederations

Simplicity also characterized the organization devised by the Mongols. Because they traveled in small groups, they did not need more than a rudimentary system of administration nor did they require a written language. Organization centered around frequently hereditary leaders, with the same surnames, who had control over people and territory. *Beki*, or shamans, conducted religious and ritual ceremonies, but leadership was generally in the hands of the patriarch, one of whose principal functions was to determine water and grazing rights for the individual families under his command. His other duties included preserving order and stability, leading his people in battle, and commanding men in hunts.

Some clans prospered while others floundered, and the prosperous ones absorbed weaker ones. These larger units, which thus encompassed more than blood relatives, necessitated a more complicated social organization, with a small "aristocracy" of clan leaders at the apex of the social hierarchy. The loyalty of these "aristocrats" to their leaders was based upon an individual and personal relationship. There was no abstract concept of loyalty to a leader. He earned his support by his achievements, by securing booty, and by maintaining close relationships with the clan leaders. As his group grew in size and power, his own income was based on regular tribute offerings from herders and extraordinary levies, often about 1 percent of the herds, in emergencies. He also organized hunts, partly to obtain food but also partly to refine the herders' fighting skills and to promote their physical conditioning.

As these units increased in size, the larger scale of warfare led to changes in social organization. A new group, known as *nököd* ("companions"), broke away from their original units and joined major leaders simply as individuals. They served as a ready reserve of armed soldiers for the leader. As his authority developed, the power of clans as political organizations eroded, and affiliation with the new group took precedence.

The religious practices of the early Mongols were also simple, but they too underwent a transformation in the late twelfth century. Because they were frequently on the move, they did not construct buildings for worship or create grandiose statues. Many worshipped or performed sacrifices on hills or mountains where *oboo*, or piles of stones, had been carefully arranged. They prayed to natural wonders such as mountains, stars, trees, fires, and rivers. These phenomena were viewed as physical representations of the supreme deity Tenggeri ("Sky God"), the Mongols' patron and protector. By the twelfth century, shamans conducted ceremonies and acted as intermediaries between the dead ancestors and Tenggeri and the living. Playing the drums, chanting, and performing dances, they made a symbolic ascent to the sky, where they communicated with the Sky God and the ancestors. They brewed up potions and recited incantations designed to cure a variety of physical ailments, and they were also reputed to be proficient in astronomy and fortune telling.

The Mongols had developed martial skills and powerful military forces before the ascendancy of Chinggis Khan. Because the women could, with little effort, assume the men's herding duties, most of the men could be mobilized for warfare. Women thus played a crucial indirect role in the Mongols' military successes. Of even greater import to the creation of a powerful Mongol military was the continuous training offered to and required of all males. Boys took part in athletics and in contests, which required endurance and physical skills, and learned how to ride horses and to shoot with a bow and arrow at a very early age. They accompanied their elders in the hunts that were designed, at least in part, as military exercises, and they learned that tight control and absolute subservience to their leaders were rigidly enforced. A typical hunt, known as a *nerge,* entailed surrounding animals over an extended distance, closing in on the animals and then shooting them. Anyone who retreated or fled was punished and often executed. This provided optimal training for battlefield discipline: retreat in this case would immediately result in execution for the soldier and sometimes for his compatriots.

When Mongols reached adulthood and were ready to join in combat, they were well equipped. They had their mounts, but they also had bows, sabers, helmets, iron-plate coverings, axes, armor, and ropes. The composite bow they used had a range of about 75 meters (246 ft.), which gave them a distinct advantage over all their rivals whose bows had a range of about 40–50 meters (131–164 ft.). On the other hand, they were not as adept in close hand-to-hand combat because they were not as skilled swordsmen as, for example, the Japanese samurai and other East Asian forces.

Mongol strategy and tactics

Mongol strategy and tactics had also become more sophisticated on the eve of Chinggis Khan's appearance as a powerful leader. One clever ploy they used was designed to give a misleading impression of Mongol strength. They placed felt puppets on horses, duping the enemy into believing that they had a much larger force than their actual number. Another successful ploy was the feigned retreat. A detachment of troops pretended to withdraw from the battlefield, and as the enemy's forces pursued them, they fell into a trap. The other detachments, which had been hiding, now suddenly appeared and surrounded and annihilated the enemy.

Some Mongol commanders added the use of psychological terror. Their forces would devastate an enemy fortress or town, massacring hundreds or thousands of people in order to frighten other enemies or cities into submitting without fighting. They would place captured enemy forces in the front lines when they initiated combat, still another devastating tactic meant to intimidate civilians into surrendering. Perhaps as important was their excellent system of intelligence. They sent agents, merchants, and native defectors to towns and oases, marketplaces and bazaars, and hostelries and caravanserais to seek information about their opponents, and hardly ever initiated a campaign without as much knowledge as they could obtain about their enemies. Eventually, they organized *yams* or postal stations every twenty miles or so to convey important military information rapidly. Maintenance of the *yams,* with provisions of horses, food, and lodgings for the riders, imposed severe burdens on the local Mongol populations. Nonetheless, riders were prepared to travel rapidly from one postal station to another to transmit vital messages. The Mongols always prepared carefully before undertaking a campaign. Supply lines, logistics, and even rudimentary medical care for the wounded were meticulously organized.

The Mongol cavalry was probably unsurpassed in its time. Both males and females had ridden horses since early childhood. They had learned to shoot a bow and arrow with deadly accuracy while riding at full speed. The endurance of both horse and rider was legendary. Cavalrymen and their beloved horses could travel quickly for days on end, either to flee a pursuing army or to conquer additional lands. They were well trained; their commanders demanded absolute obedience and expected them to follow orders conveyed by drums and other instruments during battles. The image of their galloping horses and men would eventually terrorize many countries.

What actually provoked the Mongols to initiate what turned out to be the greatest conquests in world history? One explanation is the precariousness of their economy. Droughts, cold winters, or diseases among their animals threatened their survival. Under these circumstances, they either had to trade or raid for essential goods. In addition, as they saw more of the sumptuous products of the sedentary civilizations, they began to yearn for luxuries. If they were denied commerce, they were vulnerable and might attack to obtain the products they required or coveted. By the late twelfth century, the Mongols had developed so rapidly that such attacks could devastate the settlements they chose to plunder.

The diverse groups in Mongolia were also developing and becoming more unified. The Uyghurs, a Turkic people who had resided in Mongolia until the ninth century, had migrated and created a flourishing culture in the oases of modern Northwest China. They were the first of the nomadic pastoralists in the region to develop a written language and to establish a capital city. Some had converted to the Iranian mystery religion of Manicheism and others to Buddhism. The Naimans, who inhabited the region between the Altai and the Khangai mountains in western Mongolia and thus had close contact with the Uyghurs, adopted the Uyghur alphabet and, via the Uyghurs, learned about and converted to the heretical Nestorian Christian faith. This faith asserted that Christ had two distinct identities—one as Son of God and, then, as a human son of Mary, a challenge to the central role of the Virgin Mary—and denied a co-equal Trinity because God was the progenitor and had to be superior to the Son and the Holy Ghost. The Kereyid, who inhabited the areas around the Selenge and Orkhon rivers in north-central Mongolia, had also become more organized, and many of the women had converted to Nestorianism.

In the late twelfth century, these and many other groups were fragmented. Despite similarities in their backgrounds and economies, they were not united and fought among themselves. They differed not just in their religious beliefs and their sophistication but also in their acquaintanceship with foreign cultures. Yet they faced many of the same problems, and there were sufficient similarities among them so that unity under one group or leader could make it easier to cope with these difficulties. A new force or leader was needed to end the chaos and to stabilize conditions in Mongolia.

Chapter 2
Chinggis Khan emerges

According to the *Secret History,* the last decades in twelfth-century Mongolia were often chaotic. Conflicts among different groups were bloody and damaging to the terrain. One leader after another arose to try to become the dominant figure, but no confederation developed. Divisions wracked the various regions of the country. No singular vision or ruler prevailed, leading to considerable turbulence. A disciplined, charismatic, and visionary leader was required to bring unity.

Temüjin and Mongol unity

Yisügei's son Temüjin would be that leader. The *Secret History*'s first anecdote about Yisügei is not flattering. He and several of his associates kidnapped Hö'elün, a woman affianced to a man of the Merkid people. They scared off her fiancé, and Yisügei took Hö'elün as his own wife. They subsequently conceived five children, four sons and one daughter, of whom Temüjin was the oldest. When Temüjin was eight or nine years old, his father escorted him to the encampment of Börte, the young girl to whom he had been betrothed. On his return trip, Yisügei chanced upon an encampment of Tatars, a group whom he did not recognize but who knew him, for he had killed one of their leaders. Inviting him to partake of some food and drink, they poisoned him, and he died on the way back to his own camp.

Temüjin's prospects did not seem very promising after his father's death, which prompted a return to his original household. His father's subordinates fled and left Temüjin and his family to survive on their own. At only nine years old, he could not fend for himself, but his mother, according to the *Secret History*, was the first of a remarkable group of influential women in early Mongol history. The sources portray Hö'elün as a heroic figure who saved her family and taught them the skills needed for survival, including formation of alliances with more powerful groups and rulers, in the unforgiving steppelands and the adjacent Onon River region of Mongolia. They also depict Temüjin's courageous exploits, including a hair-raising escape from captivity. However, the history does not ignore his unsavory behavior, such as the murder of his half-brother, who apparently challenged his leadership of the family. A dispute between the two brothers allegedly about the food supply escalated into a brutal and treacherous act. While his half-brother tended the family's horses, Temüjin crept behind him and shot him dead with his bow and arrow. His mother, who guessed what he had done, called Temüjin a killer and compared him to a jackal for his cowardly conduct. The *Secret History* thus presents him with blemishes, perhaps confirming its reliability as a source.

His ability to forge *anda* or blood brother relationships with wealthier or more powerful leaders was critical to his success. For example, when the Merkid captured his wife Börte, he turned to his father's *anda*, the Ong Khan of the Kereyid people, to help him recover her. In the early 1180s, their combined forces rescued his wife, who shortly thereafter gave birth to Jochi, meaning "guest," implying that the Merkid had raped and impregnated her. Nonetheless, Temüjin accepted him as one of his sons. Temüjin's *anda* Jamukha also participated in the campaign, a victory that inspired other tribes to join with Temüjin. The boost provided by this assistance from *andas* and patrons prompted him, sometime in the mid-1180s, to assume the title of Khan. He continued to collaborate with the Ong Khan against other rivals, in particular defeating the Tatars, the tribe that had murdered his father, in 1196.

Around 1202, Temüjin and the Ong Khan became enemies. The two men perceived each other as threats in their aspirations for power in the Mongol world, and the Ong Khan's son also distrusted his father's "ally" and opposed a marital alliance proposed by Temüjin. Indeed, disputes with friends and *andas* were recurring patterns in Temüjin's career. The sources often blame his former *andas* for these ruptures, a scenario that cannot always be believed. More than likely, his shifting alliances reflected his own perceptions of his position and power. He joined together with others when he needed them but dispensed with them when his forces became more powerful. He even severed his bond with Jamukha, his closest ally who had come to his rescue on several occasions.

Temüjin's struggle with the Ong Khan reveals that his drive toward total domination over the Mongols was neither preordained nor inexorable. In an initial battle in 1203, Temüjin was defeated, and he retreated to a lake where his remaining men took an oath of loyalty to him. His career appeared to be at an end. Even in these desperate circumstances, according to the sources, he insisted on sharing the limited food supplies equally with his men. After this perhaps apocryphal incident, he gathered his loyal troops, as well as men opposed to the Ong Khan, and launched a surprise attack on his previous patron, overwhelming his former benefactor's army. He then incorporated some of the Kereyid into his army. If the Ong Khan had followed up after defeating Temüjin and pursued his campaign when his rival was at his weakest, the outcome might have been different: Temüjin would not have emerged as a major figure on the Eurasian stage. This victory spurred Temüjin to challenge and then crush the Naiman people, his last opponents in Mongolia. During these battles, he captured and executed Jamukha, his most intimate *anda,* who had fought alongside the Naiman. Even so, he honored Jamukha by having him killed without the shedding of blood, a "consideration" offered only to the most esteemed enemies. Instead he had him suffocated.

As Temüjin overcame opposition, he attracted more and more men to his side. In 1206 the chiefs of the leading Mongol groups gathered together at a *khuriltai*, or assemblage of the nobility, on the banks of the Onon River to endorse Temüjin as their ruler and to grant him the title of Chinggis Khan ("Fierce ruler"). After this enthronement, Kököchü, the leading shaman among the Mongols, was to be Chinggis's sole challenger for supremacy. He wished to share power with Chinggis and sought to carve out specific realms in which he would dominate. The *Secret History* notes that Chinggis's wife Börte saw through the shaman's plans and persuaded her husband that his shaman supporter was attempting to undermine and eventually to oust him. Börte's warning doomed the shaman; Chinggis ordered his loyal aides to catch the shaman unawares and to execute him by breaking his back.

Biographers have provided a variety of explanations for Chinggis's success in unifying the Mongols, perhaps his greatest achievement. No doubt he had extraordinary charisma, which attracted many adherents. His skills as a military commander were obvious, but his administrative and political acumens were also vital. He repeatedly allied himself with more powerful commanders, offering him great credibility, and then eventually turned against them. He allegedly insisted on sharing the spoils of victory with his men. Although he was not ascetic or celibate, and indeed often took his defeated enemies' wives or concubines for his own harem, his campaigns were not motivated by a desire for an opulent lifestyle.

The organization he established contributed to unity. He divided his forces into groups of one thousand, each of which constituted a specific unit, which was then incorporated into a *tümen* or a group of ten thousand. The *tümen* served to subvert the power of the old leaders, who would be superseded by commanders loyal to and chosen by Chinggis. These commanders were not necessarily part of the old elites. Chinggis selected them on the basis of their merit and loyalty, occasionally choosing commoners who owed their positions to him and were thus even more loyal. The commanders divided up the various groups, assigning individual members to different *tümen*. They did not necessarily eliminate all earlier kinship and group allegiances, but this system certainly eroded them. Instead, individual commoners in the revised and stable units would become familiar with each other and would develop loyalty to the new groups. In return for grants of pasture land and for provision of herders to tend their animals from Chinggis, the commanders were required to collect taxes and other levies, to maintain peace in their domains, to keep their forces in fighting trim through hunts and other military exercises, and to serve in Chinggis's military campaigns when called upon to do so.

Commanders usually recruited and trained one soldier from households with two to three men, two soldiers from households with four to five men, and three soldiers from households with six to seven men. Later, censuses provided them with information for military recruitment and taxation. Most important, they were to obey Chinggis's dictates because he was the supreme ruler. Although they had jurisdiction within their own domains, they were required to accede to the tight discipline demanded by Chinggis, who did not tolerate disobedience or misbehavior. He imposed harsh punishments, including execution, on commanders and commoners who did not abide by his rules. With this system, he established centralized control over all the Mongols. Finally, as he ventured out of Mongolia, the number of non-Mongols grew and formed a vital part of his forces, still another explanation for his success.

In essence, Chinggis created a new nobility that was loyal to him. He overcame many, but not all, group and clan loyalties, and persuaded the nobles to attach themselves to the Khan. Trying to ingratiate himself, he consulted with them before undertaking large-scale military campaigns. He convened a *khuriltai* whenever he conceived of a military expedition, setting the stage for this body to assume the responsibility of ratifying or electing a new Khan. A *keshig* or new elite force of bodyguards, which he organized, further bolstered his power. Starting with a detachment of a few hundred men, the *keshig* evolved into about ten thousand who not only guarded the Khan but also cooked for him, took charge of his clothing, and prepared his weapons. Chinggis deliberately recruited some sons of the commanders for the *keshig*. This policy provided him with capable and skilled men in addition to hostages to prevent their commander fathers from contemplating rebellion.

Chinggis was also able to control Mongolian commoners and to mobilize them for his campaigns. But some of the burdens he imposed on them appeared to be excessive. They were required to leave their animals at a moment's notice to serve in military expeditions or to take part in annual hunts designed to sharpen their skills in combat. Chinggis also demanded that they pay a portion of their produce in animals or food to their overlords. Similarly, the commanders demanded extraordinary levies in times of crisis. When Mongolian leaders were about to undertake a campaign or were confronted with the need for emergency supplies in parts of their domain, they called upon commoners to contribute. Despite these impositions, most commoners remained loyal to Chinggis, who gained their support partly by providing them with booty from his conquests and partly by their fear of the consequences of not fulfilling their obligations to him.

He also sought to secure the services of foreign craftsmen, either through capturing them or enticing them through ample rewards. Because the Mongols were frequently on the move and could not count on a steady supply of raw materials, they had not developed an artisan class. However, the commanders' desire for luxuries and the construction of more permanent buildings necessitated a large group of craftsmen. Chinggis was compelled to recruit foreigners as artisans and to treat them well, often exempting them from taxation and forced labor. Later, as the territory under Mongol control expanded, he and his descendants were also required to seek the advice and assistance of foreign interpreters, engineers, and financial administrators. Like the craftsmen, these foreigners were lavishly rewarded for their services to the court.

The first group of foreigners of great importance was the Uyghur Turks, who had a written language, had settled in oases along the Silk Roads, and had thrived as merchants and craftsmen. They thus had administrative, commercial, and artistic skills that the Mongols needed. Once the Uyghurs had submitted to him in 1211, Chinggis had assistance in ruling newly subjugated domains. When he gained control over a new region, a special military unit known as a *tamma* would guarantee the peace, and a *darughachi,* or civilian governor, was assigned to administer the area. Most of the *darughachi* employed Uyghurs or other literate, capable, and experienced foreigners to help them govern. Without these foreign experts and advisers, Chinggis and his descendants would not have been able to establish a Mongol Empire.

Chinggis's foreign campaigns

A precarious economy in a demanding environment and a Chinese dynasty's denial of trade for vital products are a few of the general conditions that gave rise to the Mongol eruption from their homeland, but the specific motivations for the Mongol assault on the rest of the world are in doubt. Their military superiority is often used as an explanation for their emergence. The toughness of steppe life, according to some scholars, compelled the Mongols to be aggressive, and their aggressiveness spilled over into attacks on neighboring states. Other scholars assert that the Mongols' hunger for booty inevitably caused them to raid and assault the sedentary civilizations. Their military advantages and circumstances certainly enabled them to succeed spectacularly in the thirteenth century, but they do not explain the motives for the Mongol migrations into other lands. They tell us how the Mongols conquered much of Asia, but not why.

1. This black battle standard, one of a limited number of Mongol Empire–era articles that has survived, was used by Chinggis Khan and other Mongols on the battlefield to intimidate the enemy.

Another set of explanations relates to Chinggis himself. To prove himself to the Mongol peoples whom he had just recently subdued, he reputedly needed to embark upon far-flung campaigns against the sedentary civilizations. He allegedly believed that the Sky God Tenggeri had charged him with the responsibility of unifying and ruling the world. Yet this interpretation clashes with his policies in his three main foreign campaigns. Only in Central Asia did he maintain a large occupation force. Once he had secured his economic objectives, he withdrew from the other regions. If he had had a grand vision of world conquest, he ought to have retained total control of the other two regions in which he led military expeditions. But like other Mongols of his era, he focused on booty and trade, not on conquering and occupying land. He demanded tribute and, if necessary, troops to support him on other campaigns. His initial lack of interest in acquiring additional territory belies the conception of his fulfilling Tenggeri's command.

Another, more recent explanation is based upon climate. The proponents of this theory assert that the mean annual temperature of Mongolia declined throughout the late twelfth century. This fall in temperature probably translated into a reduction in the height and the amount of grass in the steppe land. The animals that depended on the grass were endangered, and the Mongols, who relied on their herds, were similarly threatened. Survival dictated migration out of Mongolia. The hypothesis is appealing, but it rests on premises that cannot at this time be verified. Data on the effects of low temperatures on grass are not available, nor is evidence on the relationship between declines in temperature and levels of precipitation.

In sum, the unification of the Mongol peoples, new developments in military technology, and climate may all have contributed to the Mongol onslaught. They each created conditions, which Chinggis capitalized on to become the Khan of a unified Mongol people. Chinggis himself, of course, organized the Mongols and impressed them with his vision of conquering, not merely raiding, the territories of the sedentary civilizations.

As he moved out of Mongolia to attack other regions, he invariably sent envoys to foreign rulers with so-called orders of submission. He demanded that they acquiesce to his rule, and if they did, he often allowed them to retain their own leaders as long as they offered taxes and performed the services he required. If the foreign group resisted, he initiated military campaigns. In short, he did not always thirst for war, and his successive conquests were not premeditated.

Explanations for Chinggis's and his descendants' remarkable successes are elusive. With a force initially numbering less than a million people, they carved out the largest contiguous land empire in world history. At its height, the empire stretched from Korea to Russia in the north to China to the Middle East in the south. Part of the Mongols' success was due to the decentralization and dissension that plagued many Eurasian countries. For example, three distinct and hostile, often warring, dynasties ruled China. The Southern Song, the native Chinese dynasty, governed the lands south of the Yangzi River. The Jurchens, a Tungusic people who were ancestors of the Manchus, had occupied North China in 1126, compelling the Song to abandon their capital in Kaifeng and to migrate to the southern city of Hangzhou. Establishing the Chinese-style and Chinese-influenced Jin dynasty, the Jurchens ruled much of North China but did not attract the unquestioning loyalty of their Chinese subjects. The Tanguts, a people who had affinities with the Tibetans and the Turks, had founded the Xia dynasty in Northwest China, thus dividing China into three separate regions and weakening it.

Farther to the west in Central Asia was the land controlled by the Khwarazmian shah, who faced a restive population. He and many of the rulers were Türks, but many of the inhabitants were Iranians, a source of tension and conflict. Much of the populace did not support the shah. A variety of ethnically diverse peoples inhabited modern eastern Russia and had no central government. Western Russia consisted of a number of city states, which had distinct and occasionally conflicting commercial interests. Such divisions, as well as problems with corruption and demoralization of their armies, plagued nearly all the states that the Mongols subjugated. Chinggis and his descendants simply took advantage of their weaknesses to vanquish them.

In 1209 Chinggis started his campaigns against the Tanguts and their Chinese-style Xia dynasty, partly to create a buffer zone to the west and partly because their land had great value due to its location along the trade routes to Central Asia and Iran. Claiming that the Tanguts had assisted one of the Mongol groups in its struggle with his forces, he initiated a campaign against them. However, his troops had not developed the techniques of besieging and capturing towns. When they sought to divert the Yellow River so that it would flood and cause the collapse of the walls of the Tanguts' capital city, they found, to their dismay, that their own positions were flooded as well, and they had to flee to higher ground. After several inconclusive battles, the two sides devised an unstable peace, by which the Tanguts reputedly submitted. The Tangut ruler gave his daughter to Chinggis and pledged to support the Mongols, but the Tanguts were not completely subdued.

With some control over trade routes to the west due to the alleged submission of the Tanguts, Chinggis now turned his attention to North China. In 1211, he started a four-year campaign against the Jurchen Jin dynasty, which had imposed limitations on trade with the Mongols. He defeated Jurchen troops along a wide front, and in 1214 the Jin emperor finally acquiesced and pledged to submit tribute of silk and horses to the Mongols. Shortly thereafter, the emperor moved from his capital in Zhongdu (in the area of modern Beijing) south to Kaifeng and seemed to renege on his pledge. The Mongols returned with a large force to besiege the city, a lengthy and arduous effort. Nonetheless, assisted by Chinese defectors who were experts in siege warfare and provided catapults that hurled huge rocks into the city, they finally occupied Zhongdu, the scene for a month of considerable plundering and massacres.

2. Chinggis Khan's campaigns in Central and West Asia, 1219–1225.

Chinggis stationed a few troops in the Jin areas he had subjugated but could not capitalize on his victories to occupy North China.

Instead he had to turn his attention to Central Asia. A local governor in the city of Otrar had killed a large group of Mongol and Muslim merchants, accusing them, probably accurately, of spying, and the Khwarazmian shah, 'Ala' al-Din Muhammad,

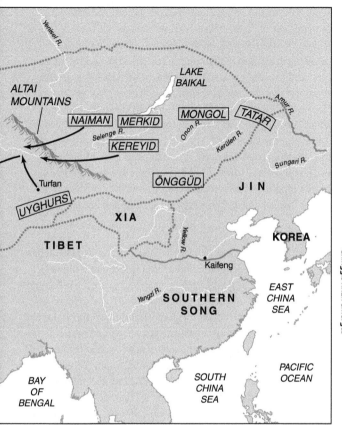

had killed one of Chinggis's envoys who had demanded that the governor be turned over to them for execution. The Mongols regarded the murder of an envoy as one of the most heinous crimes. These deaths had to be avenged. After elaborate and detailed preparations, in 1219 Chinggis, according to the sources, organized an army of two hundred thousand troops for a campaign against the shah and his domains. It remains unclear how the Mongols obtained the necessary provisions for such a large force and for the attendant number of horses in traveling through daunting deserts and lofty mountains. The shah and his forces retreated into their walled towns and awaited the Mongol army, confident that they could withstand attacks on their enclosed "fortresses." However, the Mongols had, by this time, become adept at besieging towns by using catapults and other projectiles. A five-months' siege of Otrar ended with a Mongol rout of the inhabitants. By February 1220, Chinggis had entered and razed much of the town of Bukhara. A month later, his forces, overcoming considerable resistance, moved into and destroyed part of Samarkand and deported thirty thousand artisans toward China.

If the cities had surrendered without opposition, would Chinggis have unleashed such destruction on them? It appears unlikely, though he may have deliberately wreaked havoc on the inhabitants in order to terrorize other Central Asians and to deter further opposition. Reports of these incidents intimidated the population and contributed to the Mongols' image as cruel and brutal barbarians. The Iranian historian Juvaini wrote that the Mongols "came, they sapped, they burnt, they slew, they plundered and they departed" and "with one stroke a world which billowed with fertility was laid desolate, and the regions thereof became a desert, and the greater part of the living dead, and their skin and bones crumbling dust." Another writer asserted that they killed the whole population of Herat, a major town in Afghanistan. The Iranian accounts undoubtedly inflated the number of those killed and overstated the actual destruction of cities and towns, but Central Asia had been devastated, and 'Ala' al-Din Muhammad died in 1221 while fleeing from his native land.

The Mongol army dealt a death blow to the Khwarazmian government and annexed the greatest amount of territory of any of Chinggis's campaigns. Chinggis's troops occupied cities in eastern Iran and modern Afghanistan including Balkh, Merv, and Nishapur, plundering Bamiyan and Herat as well, the first time that the Mongols had actually seized territory and sought to rule it. In his other campaigns, Chinggis had simply sought booty or favorable economic relations; his foray into Central Asia was the first indication that he wanted control over and governance of other states, a major development. Further indication of this desire was his initial efforts to build bridges, roads, and granaries, and to ensure sufficient pasture in his new domain.

Even after the Khwarazmian shah's death, his son Jalal al-Din continued to harass the Mongols until his own death in 1231. Meanwhile Chinggis had achieved his objective and in this campaign went even farther and dispatched one detachment that reached all the way to the Caspian Sea. At the same time, his other armies initiated their first assaults on Korea and cooperated with the Southern Song dynasty against the Jin rulers who controlled North China.

Chinggis himself headed toward Northwest China for his last campaign. The Tanguts, the first foreign group he had defeated, had refused to provide assistance in his struggles against the Khwarazmian shah and thus had to be punished. He arrived in Ningxia, the Tanguts' central location, but died shortly thereafter in August of 1227. A few months later, his troops overwhelmed the Xia dynasty and massacred many of the Tanguts. Chinggis had probably succumbed to old age and a demanding life, but like other great historical figures, his death and burial have become enshrouded in myths and legends. One later source attributed his death to the effects of an arrow wound during the battle with the Tanguts. Another report was that he died of injuries suffered during a hunt the previous winter. A more bizarre account states that the captured wife of an enemy leader hid a knife in her vagina and stabbed Chinggis to death during sexual intercourse.

According to later accounts, Chinggis's body was carried all the way to the Burkhan Khaldun ("Buddha Cliff") or the modern

Khentii *aimag* (province) and was buried in a secret location there, along with forty young virgins and a number of prized horses sacrificed at his grave. The Mongols deliberately concealed the precise location of his burial site to stymie grave robbers. However, many scholars question this account and argue that he was buried in the Ordos region of Northwest China, right where he died, and that only a few relics were carried back to Mongolia. They assert that the Mongols had not developed techniques of embalming and could not have transported Chinggis's body for several months, in summer heat, to the reputed grave site. Recent excavations in the supposed site in northeast Mongolia have not produced any significant results. A Japanese archaeological team found a building, grains probably from local agriculture, and evidence of a thriving iron and ceramics industry, but thus far these discoveries cannot be linked to Chinggis himself.

In addition to his administrative changes and the enlargement of territories under Mongol control, Chinggis Khan introduced other innovations, perhaps one of the more important was his policy of toleration toward foreign religions. He sought to ingratiate himself to religious leaders who might then influence their people to accept Mongol rule. His principal interest was to use religion to help him govern; he did not appear to be devoted to a specific foreign religion. He also attempted to obtain tangible benefits from religious leaders. Learning of the Chinese Daoists' efforts to develop an elixir of immortality, he invited Changchun, a Daoist sage, to accompany him on his expedition to Central Asia. However, Changchun neither dabbled in alchemy nor sought means of achieving immortality. Despite this disclaimer, Chinggis respected and consulted with Changchun, who had the temerity even to urge the Mongolian khan to refrain from taking part in hunts because heaven abhorred killing. It seems likely that Chinggis sought, through his cultivation of the Daoist sage, to win over Daoists in China. For example, he exempted Changchun's pupils and Daoist monks in general from taxation. Although he was not as generous with other religions, he did not condone any religious persecution.

His descendants generally, with a number of notable exceptions, persisted in this policy of religious toleration, but the attitudes of ordinary Mongols toward foreign religions is difficult to fathom. A few began to practice Buddhism and some converted to Islam. However, the Mongols who returned to their homeland in Mongolia after the collapse of the Mongol Empire retained the traditional shamanic rituals.

Another of his policies, which his sons and grandsons would later adopt, was the recruitment of foreign advisers and administrators to help in governing his domains. In 1204, he ordered a literate Uyghur Turk to adapt the Turkic script for its use as the first written language for Mongolian, a major step in developing a proper administration to govern the Mongol lands and other territories they would subjugate. During his expeditions in China and Central Asia, he recruited foreign soldiers, administrators, and interpreters. Yelu Chucai, one of his early recruits, assisted in devising institutions to administer the new domains brought under Mongol control. This sinicized foreigner advocated the creation of a Chinese-style administration, which Chinggis was not prepared to accept but which his sons and grandsons ultimately adopted. Nonetheless, Chinggis became a staunch supporter of greater contact with foreigners, which led his successors to recruit non-Mongols and to seek trade with foreign lands.

Still another of his policies that had profound implications was the gradual development of the *Jasagh*, guiding principles and laws that regulated the military and commoners. Chinggis continued to add to the *Jasagh* throughout his lifetime, and his decisions began to be written down while he was still alive. Because the original Mongol version has not been preserved, its contents are known only through inclusion in the works of Islamic writers. The laws concern a herding economy; an agricultural economy would require a different set of laws. There are no provisions dealing with ownership of land, the rights and duties of tenants, and the inheritance of property, the critical components of the sedentary societies Chinggis had subjugated.

Chinggis was also an ardent supporter of trade and craftsmanship. Before they erupted from Mongolia, he and fellow Mongols had needed commerce with the sedentary societies for survival. Thus he had a favorable attitude toward and fostered commerce as much as possible. His successors pursued the same policy, leading to the greatest contacts among civilizations up to that time. Similarly, the Mongols' traditional paucity of artisans prompted Chinggis to adopt supportive and benevolent policies toward them. He and his successors prized essential manufacturing items and then began to seek such luxuries as silks using gold threads or so-called cloths of gold. This patronage resulted in decorative arts explosions throughout the Mongol empire.

Chinggis's last legacy was a large and powerful military force and an astonishingly high level of violence, which turned out to be double-edged swords. His army was superior to most other contingents of troops in Eurasia. Yet its size and successes created an almost inexorable drive toward additional conquests and a yearning for more booty and greater control over more lands. What else could be done with such a large force that was primed for warfare? Its use of violence was intimidating, and it also marked a heightening of destruction during and after combat. Foreign observers and writers no doubt exaggerated the brutality of Chinggis's campaigns against the Tanguts, the Jurchens, and the Central Asians. Nonetheless, he bequeathed a tradition of violence, which accelerated as the Mongols initiated new campaigns. His attacks resulted in the indiscriminate and brutal killing of at least tens of thousands of people and in the maiming of hundreds of thousands, and the recent depiction of him as a great heroic figure and as a believer in democracy and in international law clashes with historical reality.

Chinggis's greatest accomplishment was the unification of the Mongols. He brought together herders who migrated from one area to another and roamed around a vast terrain in Mongolia, Siberia, and adjacent lands. These Mongols were accustomed to smaller units and believed that an organization of perhaps several dozen households was optimal. Chinggis expended considerable effort to persuade or compel them to form larger confederations, which proved to be the basis for their military and political successes.

Chapter 3
Conquest and governance

Before his death in 1227, Chinggis had thought about the succession to the throne. The Mongol domains, which had been expanded to include Northwest China and Central Asia, now required unified rule to foster peace and prosperity and thus riches for Chinggis' forces. He was determined that the Khanate remain in the hands of his own descendants, a judgment with which the Mongol nobility concurred. But he did not devise a structure that would facilitate a conflict-free transition from one ruler to another. He chose his son Ögödei as his successor but did not leave specific instructions for future choices, an omission that led to destructive conflicts and civil wars, which, in turn, weakened the Mongol empire.

Western campaigns

In 1227 Chinggis selected his son Ögödei to be his successor, preventing a possible struggle for rule of his domain. Yet, after his death, the Mongols did not develop a standard or orderly system of succession. They did not opt for elder brother or youngest son (ultimogeniture) succession, the traditional Mongol customs. Instead, after some initial experimentation, a *khuriltai*, whose members were the most important Mongol commanders, selected successors from the Chinggisid line. Such a procedure proved to be disastrous because different groups in the *khuriltai* supported different candidates, leading to conflict and eventually to violence. Even after endorsement by the *khuriltai,* the new ruler still had to elicit the loyalty of the nobility in order to rule. After Ögödei's death in 1241, selection by an assemblage of the Mongol nobility created fissures that weakened the empire that they had subjugated. Indeed his death may have marked the end of the empire.

All four of Chinggis's sons from his principal wife received leadership positions in his domains. Jochi, the oldest, who actually predeceased Chinggis by a few months, was granted territory north of the Khwarazmian domains stretching to the Volga River and was progenitor of the Golden Horde, which eventually ruled much of Russia. Chaghadai, Chinggis's second son, assumed control over the oases and towns of Central Asia. Tolui, the youngest son, is portrayed as the ablest military commander, but he lacked the diplomatic skills of his older brother Ögödei. Thus he was placed in charge of the Mongol homeland. All three received the title of "khan," but the supreme leader would be granted the title of "Khaghan" or "Khan of Khans."

Contemporary observers and writers, almost without exception, lauded Ögödei. The Chinese dynastic history portrayed him as considerate and generous, and as having a loyal and good heart. The Iranian historians cast him in a favorable light, noting that debtors pleaded that he cancel their debts, and he often did. They asserted that he was generous to merchants and tolerant toward Islam, Nestorianism, and other religions in his domain. He lacked the military dash of his brothers Chaghadai and Tolui, but he compensated by his abilities as a conciliator of antagonistic viewpoints and by his tolerance for different religions and groups. Yet, unlike his father, he inherited his position and did not create the kinds of personal bonds that Chinggis had developed and needed in his rise to power. Nonetheless, he was recognized as the legitimate ruler because Chinggis had chosen him, and like his father, he continued to expand into new territories. The more territories the Mongols

اوهای قاآن

تاریخ

تاریخ

شاه زادگان واراباتان

3. Ögödei, an unusually gregarious Great Khan, greets guests from his throne in this Rashid al-Din manuscript illustration.

conquered, the greater the opportunities for taxes, booty, or grazing land. In addition, the army Chinggis had set in motion required new lands to attack.

Ögödei would satisfy his armies' needs. In 1230 his forces in Central Asia would cross the Amu Darya River and head toward the eastern borders of Iran. Even closer, he initiated a campaign against the Jin dynasty, which still controlled much of northern China. With some assistance from the Song dynasty, Mongol forces compelled the Jin emperor to flee from his capital at Kaifeng in 1233; they then surrounded his troops, causing the emperor to commit suicide early in 1234. Ögödei thus occupied and had access to the material and human resources of China north of the Yangzi River, and he quickly capitalized to overwhelm both Manchuria and Korea. Another of his commanders headed toward Tibet and succeeded in compelling the Sa-skya Pandita, an important Buddhist monk, to come to his encampment. However, Tibet remained outside of Mongol control at Ögödei's death.

The Mongol campaigns farther west were the most spectacular and had the most distinguished leadership of any of the expeditions during Ögödei's reign. Chinggis's sons or grandsons took part, giving the second and third generations an opportunity to test their mettle. The hostilities and alliances generated during these campaigns in Russia and eastern Europe shaped the course of Mongol history and, in part, caused the decline and collapse of the Mongol empire. The expeditions revealed the dissension among the princely houses, with the lines of Ögödei and Chaghadai generally cooperating against those of Jochi and Tolui. Leadership was now in the hands of Jochi's son Batu, but Ögödei's oldest son, Güyüg, Chaghadai's son Büri, and Tolui's oldest son, Möngke accompanied him. The most renowned non-Chinggisid commander was Sübötei, who was perhaps the ablest military leader. According to the sources, the combined forces totaled 150,000 troops, and many were Turkic peoples, Iranians, and other subject populations—a true multiethnic army, which became characteristic of future "Mongol" troops.

The initial campaigns were resoundingly successful. The invaders from the East first crushed the Bulghars, who had established a base at the junction of the Volga and the Kama Rivers; they then overwhelmed the Kipchaks in the lower Don region, compelling the latter to flee westward to Hungary; and finally they advanced toward the Russians. In campaigns in 1237 they turned their attention to the north because they wanted to protect their northern flanks in later expeditions. The strategy that caught their enemies by surprise was their willingness to campaign in the brutal Russian winter. Mongol troops, who originated in a land plagued by even worse wintry conditions, were accustomed to the cold, and their horses were similarly inured. They surprised the Russians who believed that the weather would deter them. In fact, the Mongols capitalized on the wintry conditions. Frozen lakes and rivers enabled them readily to transport their horses and equipment.

In December 1237 Batu crossed the Volga and sent an ultimatum to the prince of Riazan, demanding one-tenth of his horses and valuables. The prince resisted, prompting Batu to lay siege to the city. Other Russian cities did not come to Riazan's assistance, leaving it vulnerable. Within a week, Batu's forces overwhelmed the defenders and plundered the city. Three months later, Mongol forces subjugated the area around Moscow and Vladimir-Suzdal and burned down the wooden buildings, facilitated by the dryness of the climate and by the lack of river or lake water, most of it iced over, to combat the flames. They then headed toward Novgorod, but the approaching spring thaw, which made the roads impassable, deterred them. After a year or two of consolidating their gains, they moved toward the major prize of Kiev. Möngke, the commander of this campaign, dispatched an envoy to Kiev to demand its submission. The Kievans responded by killing the envoy, a disastrous decision. The Mongols, in turn, responded with a devastating attack and siege, culminating in the fall of Kiev on December 6, 1240. Recent excavations of the site reveal the horrors of the campaign. One particular heart-wrenching discovery was the bodies of two young girls hiding near a stove but buried with the collapse of the city walls. Kiev, the dominant city of the pre-Mongol period, was heavily damaged, and Russia entered a new period in its history.

Having defeated Kiev, the Mongols were emboldened to campaign farther west. Novgorod, the other major commercial center of the period, had already made an accommodation with them. In 1240, its ruler Alexander had defeated the invading Swedes and the Teutonic Knights in a major battle on the frozen Neva River, from which he earned his second name of Nevsky (the Soviet director Sergei Eisenstein immortalized him in the 1938 film *Alexander Nevsky*). He did not challenge the Mongols and, in fact, permitted trade with them. In the south, by 1239, Georgia, Armenia, and Azerbaijan had submitted to the Mongols, who then conceived of an expedition against Hungary, the westernmost extension of the steppes, which could provide pasture for their horses and which had provided the Mongols with a pretext by providing sanctuary for their Kipchak enemies. Having access to the life-giving grass for their animals, the Mongols could use Hungary as a base to gain control over central Europe and then threaten western Europe. They also needed to neutralize Poland, which could, from the north, attack their troops heading toward Hungary.

Sübötei, the chief strategist for these campaigns, planned a two-pronged assault on eastern Europe. He divided his troops into five columns. Two were poised to attack Poland, two to Hungary, and one to the area of the modern Czech Republic. All five would eventually converge in an attack on Hungary. Learning about the impending invasion and of the Mongols' awesome military power, King Béla IV of Hungary appealed to the pope and the European monarchs for help, but the Europeans were divided, with Pope Gregory the IX and the Holy Roman Emperor Frederick II (r. 1220–50) especially in conflict, as Frederick challenged the papal political authority. Neither Gregory nor Frederick offered more than perfunctory assistance. Bela was on his own except for support from Polish leaders, who sought to defend their native land.

4. Mongol invasion of Russia and Eastern Europe, 1237–1242.

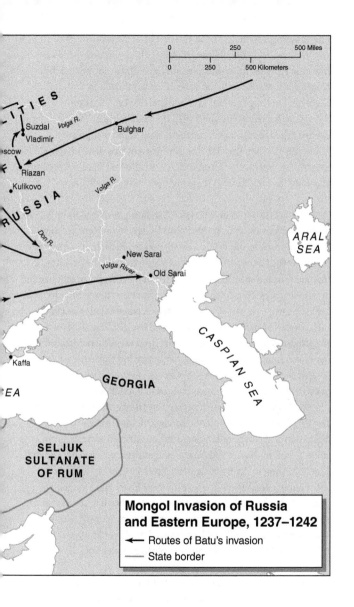

0   250   500 Miles

0   250   500 Kilometers

—ITIES

Suzdal

Vladimir

Volga R.

Bulghar

scow

Riazan

Kulikovo

Volga R.

USSIA

Don R.

ARAL SEA

New Sarai

Volga River

Old Sarai

CASPIAN SEA

Kaffa

EA

GEORGIA

SELJUK SULTANATE OF RUM

Mongol Invasion of Russia and Eastern Europe, 1237–1242

◄— Routes of Batu's invasion

— State border

The Mongols seemed to be at the height of their power, but appearances were deceptive. Hostilities had plagued the leadership from the start of the Western campaigns. Batu, supported by Tolui's sons, and Chaghadai's son Büri, supported by Ögödei's son Güyüg, were the principal antagonists. Güyüg, naturally resented Batu, who had been invested with the leadership of the campaign. Because these conflicts on occasion slowed the campaign's momentum, when Ögödei received word of this discord he recalled the principal princely commanders and allowed Batu a free hand, and Batu, in turn, sought to implement Sübotei's strategy.

One Mongol force rapidly occupied Sandomir and Cracow in Poland, prompting a reaction from the Polish leader, Duke Henry of Silesia. A Polish chronicler reports, no doubt apocryphally, that as Henry passed by the Church of the Blessed Virgin to meet the invading Mongol forces, a stone fell from the top of the church, an omen of the disaster to follow. On April 9, 1241, Henry encountered the Mongols near the town of Legnica. The two sides seemed evenly matched, with each consisting of about seven thousand to eight thousand soldiers. Knowledge of the terrain and support from the local population could have been significant advantages for Henry, but the battle actually favored the Mongols. The Polish-German forces anticipated hand-to-hand combat, but the Mongols instead flooded them with a barrage of arrows. With scant armor for protection, the troops were vulnerable. The Polish sources attribute the Mongol victory to their use of divination and witchcraft. Henry himself suffered a wound from a lance, fell off his horse, and was quickly surrounded and decapitated. Also according to the Polish sources, the Mongols cut off the ears of the enemy dead and filled up nine large bags. The Mongols then headed toward Legnica, whose inhabitants refused to surrender and mounted a stiff resistance, which caused the invaders to withdraw. The Mongols later initiated half-hearted punitive campaigns in 1259–60 and 1287–88, but were unable to conquer Poland.

Having defused the threat from Poland, Batu could now concentrate on Hungary, the real prize of his eastern European campaign. On April 11, 1241, Batu himself led his army on a successful surprise attack against Béla at the town of Muhi. Béla's troops were utterly vanquished, and he barely managed to escape. Mongol forces pursued the Hungarian king into Dalmatia but were unable to capture him. In December 1241 the Mongols swept southwestward, seized Pesth, and traversed the frozen Danube to capture and destroy the town of Buda.

Once the Mongols had occupied much of Hungary, an attack on western Europe seemed inevitable. Moreover, the secular and religious authorities in the West were too busy squabbling among themselves to consider concerted action against the marauders. A divided Europe seemed to be ripe for conquest. Yet the Mongols halted in eastern Europe and, in fact, began to withdraw. In May 1242 Batu led his troops back to Russia where he established his capital in Sarai on the lower Volga. One possible motive for Batu's precipitous withdrawal may have been the dearth of grasslands for the Mongolian horses, as western Europe offered little pasture for his steeds. His animals had consumed much of the grass in the Hungarian steppes, which needed to recover and to be replenished after the demands made on it by the invaders from the East. Another motive may have been the death of the Great Khan Ögödei on December 11, 1241. Ögödei's death meant that the Mongol nobility needed to convene a *khuriltai* in its ancestral homeland to select a new Great Khan. Batu, as the oldest member of the second generation of Mongol rulers, ought to attend these meetings and to participate in the deliberations. However, he did not return to Mongolia and did not take an active part in the election. Still another motive may have been that the Mongol-led forces had suffered substantial casualties in the Western campaigns and did not have the resources, both in manpower and supplies, to advance any farther.

Ögödei's death may have saved Western Europe from the wrath of the Mongol invaders, but his reign nonetheless witnessed a remarkable expansion of territory. The Mongols seized most of

China north of the Yangzi River, imposed their authority over Korea and Manchuria, subjugated Azerbaijan, Georgia, and Armenia, and made their first foray into Iran. They conquered much of Russia and campaigned successfully in Hungary and Poland. Their military successes terrorized Asia and Europe and helped create the largest contiguous land empire that the world had ever seen.

Governing an empire

Territorial expansion was not the only achievement of Ögödei's reign. He overcame great pressure from Mongol traditionalists from North China to convert these territories into grasslands and establish the kind of economy to which they were accustomed. Instead, the Great Khan began to set up institutions to rule his vast domain. He recruited the able official Yelu Chucai, who had also served his father, to assist him in devising a rudimentary administration. Yelu, who became chief minister for a time, prevented the devastation of the Chinese countryside and its conversion to grazing areas, arguing that revenues derived from promotion of agriculture would exceed any income derived from herding in unsuitable land.

Then he revised the Mongol system of taxation to fit the requirements of the sedentary civilization in China. Recognizing that peasants needed regularity in the determination of their financial obligations, he proposed a head tax on male adults, a tax on land based on size and fertility, and a levy calculated on the number of oxen and farm tools; in order to satisfy the Mongols' demands for tangible items other than grain, the taxes would often be paid in silver and silk. He pledged that significant amounts of grain, silver, and silk would accrue to the Mongols if the Great Khan implemented this system. Finally, his proposed tax on commerce, which the Mongols labeled *tamgha*, promised additional revenue. In 1235 Ögödei ordered that a census be conducted, facilitating the imposition of these taxes, as well as providing information used for military recruitment. By 1236 a fairly reliable census, the first in the newly subjugated lands of North China, provided Ögödei with the tools required for the new state's need for revenue and an army. Because Ögödei had just commissioned the campaign against Russia and eastern Europe, an accounting, via Yelu's proposed census of resources at his command, was essential.

Yelu proved unable to impose his system of tax collection. He proposed the establishment of tax collection bureaus manned by government officials, but his opponents, who recognized that Ögödei's campaigns and construction projects were costly, advocated a system of tax farming. Under this system, merchants, many of them Central Asian Muslims, would be granted licenses to collect taxes. As private entrepreneurs, the merchants' primary interest would be to maximize profits. Eager for this added income, Ögödei eventually sided with the advocates of tax farming, at the risk of alienating the native, mostly Chinese, population.

Yelu's proposals for an administrative structure were also not accepted. He sought to restore a regular Chinese-style organization, with officials chosen through the traditional civil service examinations, which emphasized knowledge of Confucianism. Ögödei permitted a civil service examination, but most of the successful candidates served principally as advisers or were appointed to minor posts. Yelu then tried to persuade Ögödei to have Confucian scholars tutor their Mongol overlords. The Great Khan agreed, but it is hard to believe that many of the Mongol princes and nobles grasped the concepts to which they were exposed. Yelu's efforts to devise a system of local administration also failed. Instead Ögödei granted lands for the maintenance of his relatives and the nobility, which permitted them to govern local regions throughout the empire. He also transformed *darughachi*, originally a military title, into a civilian title for administrators of newly incorporated territories.

Opposition to Yelu's attempted accommodations to the subjugated Chinese population mounted among some Mongols, Uyghur Turkic government officials, and Muslim tax collectors and merchants. At last, Turkic officials, allied with Muslim tax collectors, finally eclipsed his influence in government.

In one cooperative venture, Yelu and the Turkic officials persuaded the khan to build a permanent capital city, an indication that the Mongols would actually seek to rule from an administrative center rather than simply engage in plunder. Ögödei chose Khara Khorum, in the center of the old Mongol domains, as the site for his capital. After ordering workmen to build a wall and watchtowers surrounding the city, Ögödei had his own relatively elaborate palace, known to the Chinese as the *Wanangong*, built within the walls and then constructed palaces for the imperial princes adjacent to his own. Several decades elapsed before the construction of this elaborate city in the grasslands was completed. A north–south road leading to the center of Khara Khorum reveals the importance of trade to the city. Ögödei's subjects also built two

5. A statue of a tortoise, a Chinese motif, is one of the few remaining objects from the ancient Mongol capital of Khara Khorum. A Chinese army destroyed the capital in the fourteenth century.

mosques, Buddhist and Daoist temples, and a Nestorian Christian church within the city.

Craftsmen from China, Central Asia, Iran, and as far away as Europe fashioned essential as well as luxury products. Khara Khorum's ethnic diversity has been documented through the discovery of Chinese roof tiles, roof ridge ornaments, a gold bracelet and ceramics, silver coins and cenotaphs with Arabic inscriptions, Indo-Nepalese Buddhist figures, and a silver drinking fountain built by a Frenchman. Archaeologists have recently discovered the site of a Buddhist temple with fragments of a wall painting adorned with Indo-Nepalese, Chinese, Tibetan, and Tangut motifs, further evidence of the diverse ethnicity of its inhabitants. They have also excavated areas for production of glass, gems and precious stones, and bone carving, as well as furnaces for smelting of metals, especially bronzes. Although William of Rubruck, a European missionary to the Mongols, was not impressed and compared it unfavorably to the small Parisian section of St. Denis, Khara Khorum was a remarkably cosmopolitan site, particularly for a city in the grasslands.

Yet William proved somewhat prescient in recognizing that Khara Khorum was not ideally situated as the capital of a great empire. The city and the neighboring regions could not provide basic provisions for its increasing population. The inhabitants also devoted considerable effort to water management. Although Khara Khorum was near the Orkhon River, a growing population placed enormous strains on the city's water supply. It was indeed an artificial city because it did not lie along a major trade route, had little arable land, and was not near a vital source of raw materials. The city was also distant from the key economic centers of Ögödei's domains. China, Central Asia, and Russia were more productive than this relatively isolated location on the empire's fringes. William of Rubruck writes that four hundred carts arrived daily to supply the city, a costly and inefficient system. In short, its location was an albatross on the Mongol empire. The Mongols had chosen the site because it symbolized their attachment to their homeland, but it was simply unsuitable as a capital city for a growing empire, which required an ever increasing bureaucracy. Three decades elapsed before a Great Khan moved the capital to a more tenable site.

Two women and the Great Khanate

Ögödei's reign witnessed major developments for the Mongols but also revealed problems that would bedevil them. The Mongols devised a tax system, began to set up governmental institutions, and built a capital, all of which were required if they were to govern the lands they had subjugated. They laid a firm foundation for the efforts of the third generation of the Chinggisid clan to rule a diverse multiethnic domain.

However, a telling indication of the Mongols' problems was a five-year interregnum between Ögödei's death in 1241 and the enthronement of his successor. Unlike his father, Ögödei had not chosen a successor, thus permitting an assemblage of the Mongol nobility to select the most meritorious leader in the Chinggisid line. Ögödei's descendants would surely have an advantage, particularly since the lines of his brothers Chaghadai and Jochi and their progeny were preoccupied with maintaining control over Central Asia and Russia respectively. Based on the principle of ultimogeniture, the descendants of his youngest brother Tolui's descendants had legitimate claims to the position of Great Khan. Tolui's widow, Sorghaghtani Beki, was determined to place one of her sons on the throne. Chinggis had captured her after defeating the Ong Khan and had given her in marriage to his son.

Foreigners from within and beyond the Mongol empire lauded Sorghaghtani Beki for her extraordinary abilities. The Iranian historian Rashid al-Din, for example, proclaimed her to be the most intelligent and able woman in the world. Married to Tolui, who died at an early age, she turned her attention to the territory in North China, which Ögödei had granted for her support. She recognized that ravaging of the mostly agricultural land and plunder of the area's resources would be disastrous policies. Tax revenues would increase if she fostered the native agrarian economy instead of imposing a Mongolian-style pastoral economy.

Her other policies and activities reveal a similar farsightedness. For example, although she was a fervent Nestorian Christian, she provided help to the major Chinese religions, Buddhism and Daoism, in order to ingratiate herself with the Chinese in her new domain in North China. The Iranian historians also note approvingly that she offered alms to poor Muslims, rewarded their leaders, and contributed funds for the building of mosques and madrassahs or theological colleges. She recognized that support from clerics would facilitate her efforts to rule. Equally important was her supervision of the education and training of her four sons, for all of whom she had lofty ambitions.

Like Eleanor of Aquitaine, Sorghaghtani Beki reared four sons who became monarchs. She was determined that they first learn about and follow the dictates of the traditional Mongol customs and codes. All four learned to ride and shoot with bows and arrows, and found great pleasure in hunting; hunting continued to be an important motif throughout their lives. In addition, Sorghaghtani was determined that they be literate. For example, she recruited a Uyghur named Tolochu to teach her son Khubilai to read and write the recently developed Mongol written language. She also sought a multiethnic group of advisers to tutor her sons and to expose them to the concerns of the sedentary world. In short, her sons were well equipped to become rulers.

Ögödei's widow, Töregene, barred the way to the succession. Both she and Sorghaghtani Beki had legitimate claims for the Great Khanate for one of their sons. Töregene's husband had been the Great Khan and could claim a father-son succession, while Sorghaghtani was the widow of Tolui, Chinggis Khan's youngest son, and, by the traditional Mongol custom of ultimogeniture, ought to have been selected as the Great Khan. Now Tolui's children could, based on their father's claims, contest the succession. Töregene sought to place her son Güyüg on the throne, while Sorghaghtani was equally determined to enthrone her oldest son Möngke. Ögödei's widow initially had the upper hand because her husband had been the Great Khan. Capitalizing on her status as the Great Khan's widow, she assumed the position of regent for four years until Güyüg, who had participated in the campaigns in Russia, was ready to assume the title of Great Khan.

The struggle for the Great Khanate in the 1240s reflected a conflict between two conceptions of governance. Töregene represented the traditional Mongol customs and appeared primarily interested in exploitation of the conquered regions. She sought to enrich herself and her fellow Mongols, and granted domains to Mongol commanders without devising new institutions to govern the recently subjugated sedentary populations. On the other hand, Sorghaghtani Beki recognized that success required an accommodation with her subjects, who were mostly Chinese peasants, and was willing to use their institutions to govern them. The conflict interrupted the Mongols' military campaigns, except for their defeat in 1243 of the Seljuk Turks, their first encroachment into Anatolia.

Töregene had her way: her son Güyüg was enthroned as the Great Khan in 1246. More than four thousand envoys from all corners of the Mongol domains, as well as a European papal emissary named John of Plano Carpini, attended the coronation. As soon as he took power, Güyüg swept away most of his mother's cohorts, torturing and killing, in particular, many of her Muslim associates. He relied instead on Nestorian Christians to help him rule his vast domains. Unlike his father, he established his residence in the steppelands instead of in Khara Khorum, the capital his father had constructed. This step signaled the beginnings of a rupture between the Mongols who espoused the traditional values and those who recognized the need to accommodate to the sedentary societies of the conquered populations in order to rule them, a conflict that would weaken the Mongols.

Güyüg's reign witnessed the first direct contact between a Great Khan and Europeans; several of the European monarchs and the pope, concerned about the Mongols' conquests reaching all the way to Hungary, sought to defuse the possibility of a Mongol attack. The Europeans had also been dazzled by the myth of a benevolent and magnanimous Christian monarch named Prester John, who allegedly had once ruled the Mongols. However, the Europeans themselves were divided, with the Holy Roman Emperor and the pope the chief antagonists. Nonetheless, at an Ecumenical Council convened in Lyons in 1245, the pope and the secular leaders decided to dispatch an embassy to the Mongols. The Franciscan monk John of Plano Carpini led this mission and delivered two papal letters demanding that the Mongols abandon their military campaigns in the West and urging them to convert to Christianity. Infuriated by these haughty letters, Güyüg, in turn, demanded that the European monarchs and the pope submit to the Mongols. Neither side gained anything from this diplomatic confrontation.

Meanwhile the tensions that had been brewing in the Mongol imperial family erupted. Güyüg and his cousin Batu, the khan of the Golden Horde in Russia, had been at odds for many years, and in 1247 Güyüg, claiming that he was heading for the more healthful climate of Central Asia, set forth with his troops to attack Batu's camp. Learning of Güyüg's intentions, Sorghaghtani Beki saw an opportunity to ingratiate herself with the ruler of Russia and warned Batu, a dangerous move that could have led to her execution. Fortunately for her, Güyüg died en route, and she thus won over a valuable ally in Batu.

The houses of Tolui and Ögödei, with the Chaghadai Khanate in Central Asia supporting Ögödei, now officially contended for the throne in the first violent confrontation between the descendants of Chinggis Khan. Both sides feverishly rallied for the support of the Mongol nobles who would shortly assemble in a *khuriltai* to elect a new ruler. For some years, Sorghaghtani Beki had been ingratiating herself with these notables by providing them with gifts and honors, and she had Batu's undying support. In February 1251 the Mongol nobility compensated her for her efforts and enthroned Sorghaghtani's son Möngke as the Great Khan. Sorghaghtani Beki lived long enough to enjoy her victory, but not enough to obtain personal profit from her efforts. In the first month of 1252 (February 12–March 11), she succumbed. She had provided her four sons, Möngke, Khubilai, Hülegü, and Arigh Böke, with the training necessary to rule sedentary civilizations. Their consorts, whom she had helped to select, were generally clever and supportive, and their religious toleration, which she had helped to nurture, would serve them well in governing the diverse peoples in the Mongol lands. To demonstrate their gratitude, her sons erected a number of tablets in her honor both in Daidu (the name of the eventual Mongol capital in Beijing) and in Zhendingfu, the seat of her first domain. In 1335 her portrait was hung in a Nestorian church in the North Chinese town of Ganzhou. But the portrait was lost, destroyed, or stolen, and no image of this remarkable woman has survived.

The house of Tolui emerges

Möngke had become the Great Khan, but his opponents had not renounced their claims. A bloody conflict would ensue, leading to imprisonment, purges, and murders. These struggles marked the end of a unified Mongol empire. The various territories subjugated by the Mongols would begin to fragment into autonomous, occasionally warring states. Because the available primary sources (the Chinese official history of the Mongol dynasty and Rashid al-Din's universal history) represented the interests of the winners in this struggle, it is difficult to reconstruct the events in an unbiased way. These accounts portray Möngke's adversaries as disloyal schemers bent on personal profit.

Möngke's reprisals for disloyalty were swift and terrible. His officials wrapped Güyüg's widow in felt and drowned her. Two of Möngke's cousins were decapitated. In short, many of Ögödei's descendants and their supporters were executed, exposing the first real fissures in the Chinggisid line. Surprisingly, Ögödei had been extremely helpful to his nephew Möngke. He had assisted in selecting Möngke's principal wife and had chosen his nephew specifically to participate in the Western campaigns. Yet Möngke turned against his patron's relatives in his rise to power, fulfilling his mother's ambitions to groom a Great Khan.

Möngke's policies were, in many ways, modeled on those of earlier Mongol rulers. Like his predecessors, Möngke was tolerant of the religions in his domains, though he himself probably remained a believer in shamanism. And like his uncle Ögödei, he recruited an international coterie of advisers and officials. In 1252 he ordered his scribes to conduct a census of the population throughout his domains. Over the next few years, he authorized other censuses. Once these registrations were completed, he began to develop a tax system that provided sufficient revenue but was regular and not as onerous and capricious as those of the earlier khans. These stable and fixed taxes would lessen the individual burdens, particularly on peasants. Möngke also restricted the exactions imposed by Mongol nobles, demanding that only the court impose military service, taxes, and forced labor. The need for registration of the population was prompted by his drive for a planned renewal of expansionist campaigns. With proper resources, his armies were poised for expeditions as far-flung as the Russian and eastern European campaigns. The censuses would facilitate the recruitment of men for the military, the imposition of forced labor—especially ensuring a corps of attendants at postal stations, which dispatched messages speedily to the various armies—and funds to supply the expeditions. Finally, Möngke tried to prevent disunity by demanding that the other Chinggisid lines transmit taxes from their domains and provide troops for military campaigns, but this objective proved to be elusive. His three brothers acquiesced, but his other relatives did not abide by his orders, although no major civil war erupted during his reign.

With such relative tranquility, he could pursue the expansionism that had become characteristic of the Mongols. He assigned his brothers to the primary operations, Hülegü to conquer West Asia and Khubilai to participate in a campaign against China's Southern Song dynasty. Möngke instructed his brothers to avoid unnecessary violence and destruction. He had learned from his mother that annihilation of conquered peoples and disruption of their economies were unsound policies. The Mongols could collect more taxes from a flourishing economy that produced considerable revenue.

When the Great Khan Möngke assigned his brother Hülegü to attack West Asia, did he intend occupation, control, and establishment of a new government, which the Mongol rulers of Central Asia and Russia could perceive to be a threat? Or was Hülegü commissioned merely to subjugate the region including Iran, to the west, and then return to East Asia? He would actually start his own dynasty, a step that resulted in conflicts with the Mongol dynasties in both Russia and Central Asia. The Golden Horde and the Chaghadai rulers believed that Chinggis had provided them with jurisdiction over the areas to the west of China, including Iran and the other Middle Eastern lands. They considered Iran and West Asia as part of their potential spheres of influence. These differing perceptions set the stage for battles among the various Mongol khanates, conflagrations that would contribute to the collapse of the Mongol domains.

Hülegü's campaigns suggest that he had received Möngke's blessing to create a new khanate in West Asia. First, he was deliberate in his preparations. His slow pace and the considerable attention he paid to intelligence and logistics indicate that he did not perceive this foray as a hit and run raid. Such elaborate groundwork bolsters the view that he intended to occupy, not just plunder, the regions he conquered. Second, his successful efforts at recruiting Turks and Iranians into his military forces offer additional proof that he did not seek simply to devastate West Asia and then retreat to East Asia. He must have recognized that a goal of total destruction would alienate his multiethnic forces. Third, he constructed bridges and roads, with the assistance of local inhabitants, as his troops traveled westward and after they seized Iran and parts of the Middle East, an indication that he attempted to build, rather than totally ravage, the lands he seized. To be sure, these transport improvements facilitated the army's march westward. Yet Hülegü repeatedly ordered renovation or construction of buildings after pacification of a region was complete.

With Möngke's instructions in mind, Hülegü prepared cavalry and Chinese engineers and other specialists in siege warfare for the campaign in the Middle East. Ignoring accusations of laxity and lugubriousness, he devoted considerable effort to training his troops, gathering information about his enemies, and ensuring his supply lines for both men and animals. Because his wife was an ardent Nestorian Christian, he courted the Christians en route. King Het'um I of Lesser Armenia, who had just returned from a visit to Khara Khorum during which he kept an invaluable diary of his travels, was impressed with the Mongols' apparent commitment to Christianity and sent auxiliary troops for the campaign. In fact, Hülegü never became a Christian and instead had specific political objectives. He aimed to expand the territories under Mongol control, and his expeditions were not crusades against Islam. Nonetheless, Het'um I instructed his son-in-law Bohemund VI of Antioch to assist the invaders from the East.

Hülegü's first campaign was directed at the Nizari Ismaili order of Shi'i Islam, which is misleadingly known as the Order of the Assassins. The Ismailis, who claimed descent from Muhammad's son-in-law Ali, occupied parts of eastern Iran and had established a secure base at the fortress of Alamut, in the Elburz Mountains south of the Caspian Sea, from which they withstood attacks from Sunni enemies and from the Abbasid Caliphate in Baghdad. Their secretiveness and their support of violence had alienated large segments of the western and Central Asian populations and had aroused much opposition. A relatively small group, they occasionally relied on assassinations of their adversaries' leaders. Pledging entrance to paradise to recruits who undertook such suicide missions, their leader had developed a negative image in Asia. The Ismailis could not and did not receive assistance when Hülegü reached Alamut. In fact, the Iranian historian Juvaini praised Hülegü and the Mongols for their attack on the Ismailis. Although he recognized the value of their library and helped to save it, he still reflected the prevailing antagonism toward the Ismailis. In 1256 the Mongol troops bombarded the seemingly impregnable Ismaili fortress with stone missiles, primitive rockets, and explosive devices, finally breaking down its defenses and causing its Grand Master, Rukn al-Din, to surrender. According to Islamic sources, Hülegü exacted a terrible price on the Ismailis. Many were slaughtered, and Rukn al-Din and his entire family were killed.

Similarly, many in the declining Abbasid domains, which controlled Iran and much of West Asia, had turned against the caliphate in Baghdad because of what they perceived to be political oppression and corruption. It is perhaps too much of an overstatement to assert that they viewed Hülegü as a savior and welcomed him as a king, but no doubt dissatisfaction with the Abbasids attracted many Turks, Iranians, and Arabs to his side and somewhat facilitated his conquests.

The same fate befell the Abbasid capital at Baghdad. The Abbasid caliphate, the dominant Islamic dynasty after about 750, had declined precipitously since its heyday at the time of Harun al-Rashid and could not resist the invaders from the East. The Mongol invaders received considerable assistance from Iranians who wanted to subvert Arab supremacy in the caliphate. Iranian experts assisted with the catapults and other siege engines located along the city gates. After ten days of battle early in 1258, Baghdad submitted and was sacked, and the Abbasid caliph was killed. The sources differ about the circumstances of his death. One version has him locked in a prison surrounded by his gold and starved to death. Another version is that molten gold was poured down his throat. The likeliest scenario is that he was wrapped up in a felt rug and his body was crushed by the Mongols' horses to prevent the spillage of blood, the Mongols' "honorable" and usual method of executing enemy rulers.

Parts, but not all, of the city were devastated. One source estimated that the dead numbered eight hundred thousand and another at two million, undoubtedly exaggerated figures. Still another account refers to twelve thousand ears submitted to Hülegü as well as massacres of unarmed civilians after they had surrendered. It adds that the dead could not be buried for some time because of the lack of space in the makeshift cemeteries and the insufficient number of men available to carry and dispose of the corpses. With the warm weather of spring and summer arriving, the stench from the putrefying bodies enveloped the city. A cholera epidemic, affecting both the inhabitants of Baghdad and the Mongol invaders, contributed to the losses incurred during the campaign. However, within a decade or so, travelers again referred to Baghdad as a great commercial center, challenging the reports about the Mongols' total devastation of the city. The Mongols had been brutal but not self-destructive. They would not totally devastate an area that could be a valuable source of income.

On the one hand, Hülegü's capture of Baghdad, the Abbasid capital, and his continued march westward persuaded the Mongol rulers in Russia and Central Asia that he intended to remain in the West, opening a rift in the Mongol world. On the other hand, the Mongols' destruction of the caliphate, a devastating blow for the Islamic world, revived European hopes of a better relationship with the conquerors from the East who had dealt a death blow to the caliphate, one of the

6. Hülegü Khan's attack on Baghdad shows the powerful siege engines required to overwhelm the city. Such sieges reveal the Mongols' increasing reliance on sophisticated weaponry rather than simply on cavalry.

crusaders' Muslim enemies. The initial contacts, however, were not successful. The Franciscan monk William of Rubruck, an unofficial emissary sent by King Louis IX of France, had traveled to Mongolia in 1253 not only to cement good relations but also to gather as much information as he could. He succeeded in learning a great deal about the Mongols, which he set forth in one of the best accounts about them. However, like John of Plano Carpini, he failed in his other task of establishing more cordial relations. Möngke gave William a letter setting forth the Mongol claim of universal rule and demanding that the French monarch send official envoys to indicate his acceptance of a subordinate status.

Nonetheless, Hülegü's campaigns against the Ismailis and the Abbasids inspired European hopes of an alliance against the Muslims who still controlled the Holy Lands. Several European monarchs, as well as the pope, continued to envision another Crusade to recapture these important Christian sites. They faced a formidable obstacle in the Mamluks, a newly arisen Turkic dynasty based in Egypt, and hoped to collaborate with the Mongols against this Islamic force. But a year after Hülegü's victory in Baghdad, the Mongol world was plunged into still another succession crisis. This turning point in Mongol history was shaped by the relationship between the Great Khan and his two younger brothers, Khubilai and Arigh Böke.

Chapter 4

The Mongols and the world: part 1

By the end of Möngke's reign and the accession of Khubilai Khan as the Great Khan in 1260, the Mongols had carved out a vast east–west empire stretching from Korea to Iraq and Russia. The khans in all these regions had decided to rule rather than to devastate and extort goods from the territories they had subjugated. The various regions would fragment into four, occasionally warring, khanates, but communication and commerce among them persisted. The Mongols' original homeland and north China and Korea constituted one khanate, and Central Asia, Russia, and West Asia were the three others. The four shared some policies, but each also adopted and adapted practices and government agencies from the people they ruled.

Despite their differences and conflicts, the various khanates controlled much of Asia and fostered economic, technological, and artistic relations among the continent's regions. The array of travelers lends credence to the view that the Mongol period was the onset of global history. A number of these voyagers wrote invaluable accounts of the regions in Eurasia they visited. Marco Polo was the most famous of these travelers, but the Muslim jurist Ibn Battuta, the Nestorian Christian Rabban Sauma, the Armenian King He'tum, the Franciscans John of Plano Carpini and William of Rubruck, and the Chinese Confucian Zhou Daguan, among others, described sites from Angkor Wat to Hangzhou to Tabriz to Paris. These travelers journeyed along the traditional land-based Silk Roads, which the Mongols revived after a lapse of several centuries, as well as the sea routes from West, South, and Southeast Asia to southern Chinese ports.

The early career of Khubilai Khan

Khubilai Khan is the ruler most often associated with the cosmopolitanism that began to prevail among some of the Mongols. While his younger brother Hülegü expanded the Mongol-controlled territories in West Asia, Khubilai asserted himself in East Asia. Almost nothing is known of his early life except for a seemingly stereotyped account of his first successful kill of an animal during a hunt in which he had accompanied his grandfather Chinggis. In the 1240s, Khubilai had focused on ruling the territory in North China he had been granted as his domain. Chinese, Muslim, Mongol, and Tibetan counselors and officials helped him to govern these lands. Like his mother Sorghaghtani Beki, he gradually recognized that stable rule over China required accommodation with Chinese institutions and practices. Thus he fostered the agrarian economy, by constructing irrigation works and providing improved tools and seeds, rather than imposing a pastoral economy on the Chinese, and he ordered his officials to devise a regular and stable tax system for the peasants.

In July 1252, his brother Möngke gave him an order that required further involvement with Chinese affairs. The Great Khan commanded him to bring the kingdom of Dali, in the present-day province of Yunnan, under Mongol control. Dali was fortuitously located along the trade routes to Burma and South Asia and could also be a strategic base from which to launch an attack on Southern Song China, the Mongols' principal enemy in East Asia. Khubilai made elaborate preparations for the campaign. Before setting

7. **Mongol khanates, 1280.**

forth, he dispatched three envoys to demand the submission of Dali. Instead, the leading minister executed the emissaries.

Khubilai assumed that a bloody war would be needed to compel Dali to capitulate, but Yao Shu, a Confucian scholar who accompanied him, may have prevented such loss of life and severe damage. To try to prevent further bloodshed, Yao proposed that the Mongols send a detachment to Dali with

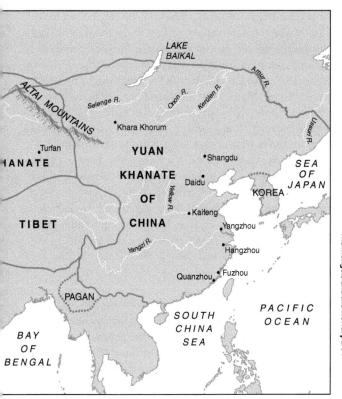

banners proclaiming that they would not wantonly kill and loot. For some decades, the Mongols had used the tactic of pledging not to destroy a town if its inhabitants surrendered peacefully. Dali submitted, and Khubilai fulfilled his pledge: only those who executed his envoys were put to death. He did not alter the system of government and simply demanded taxation and an opportunity to use Dali's territory as a base for an eventual campaign against the Southern Song.

After returning to his lands in North China, he planned to set up a regular administrative system. With the counsel of Chinese and foreign advisers, he supported agriculture and commerce, fostered education, devised a tax system, and recruited his own forces. He turned for assistance to Liu Bingzhong, a Buddhist monk well versed in Confucianism and talented in mathematics, astronomy, calligraphy, and painting. Liu had earlier prepared a lengthy memorandum consisting of specific recommendations for governance, which presumed a return to a traditional Chinese system. He advocated the restoration of ancient Chinese rituals and ceremonies, and the institution of regular legal and tax structures that did not overburden Khubilai's subjects, and the nurturing of scholar-officials through the reintroduction of the civil service examinations. Khubilai adopted all these proposals except for the restoration of the civil service examinations, which would result in overreliance on Chinese officials.

The most important signal of his intentions was his construction of a capital city, which identified him with the sedentary lifestyle of the Chinese and attested to his desire to govern his Chinese domains. The capital, situated in Inner Mongolia, was known originally as Kaiping but eventually renamed Shangdu (Upper Capital); Khubilai selected it as the center of his government by the use of the ancient Chinese principles of *fengshui* or geomancy—a divination scheme designed to find the most propitious location for construction of residences, tombs, and other structures. The capital, which Marco Polo dubbed "Ciandu" and became "Xanadu" in Samuel Taylor Coleridge's poem "Kubla Khan," was well planned. A walled city on the Chinese model, it supported a population of approximately one hundred thousand people. The Outer City boasted Buddhist and Daoist temples, and the Inner City's most distinctive building was the marble Imperial Palace, which Marco Polo described in detail. He wrote that "the halls and rooms . . . are all gilded and wonderfully painted . . . with pictures and images of beasts and birds and trees and flowers . . . so well that it is a delight and a wonder to see." These various structures, in design and in use of motifs, were similar to those found in earlier Chinese cities. The main addition was a park outside the Outer City that was used for hunting and falconry, and represented the principal Mongol touch.

Khubilai's policies and his apparent Chinese orientation aroused the concern of Mongol traditionalists, but Möngke, after a few initial misunderstandings, trusted his younger brother and commissioned him to deal with disputes between Buddhist and Daoist monks, one of the knottiest problems facing the empire in North China. Violence had erupted between the two religions, as each side attacked the other's vulnerable monasteries. Power and status rather than doctrinal disputes generated hostility. The two religions shared some beliefs, and indeed the earliest translators of the Buddhist writings into Chinese had used Daoist terminology to identify important Buddhist concepts. Buddhists and Daoists came into conflict over land, tangible property, and a desire for government patronage, and the arguments each used against the other had scant relation to ideology. The Buddhists claimed that the historical Buddha predated Laozi, the reputed founder of Daoism, and that the Indian sage's earlier birth signified his superiority over the Chinese philosopher. The Daoists countered that Laozi had traveled to the "Western Regions," the Chinese term for Central Asia and India, after expounding the pure form of his teaching in China. He then transformed himself into one of his many emanations, became known in India as the Buddha, and developed the Buddhist doctrine, a corrupt and simplistic form of his teachings for the less sophisticated peoples of the Western Regions.

In 1258 Khubilai convened a conference of the leading Buddhists and Daoists in East Asia to debate the contentious issues that separated them. By this time, Khubilai leaned toward Buddhism. The Great Khan had been impressed by the Tibetan Buddhist monk 'Phags-pa, who was instructing Khubilai's wife Chabi, and

Khubilai had himself received religious instruction from the twenty-three-year-old Tibetan monk. From the beginning, he sided with the Buddhists, but he offered the Daoists one chance to redeem themselves. He demanded that they perform such magical and supernatural feats as curing illnesses, changing the weather, and foretelling the future, in which they reputedly claimed to be proficient. Unable to demonstrate any otherworldly powers, the Daoists could not meet the challenge. Khubilai then declared that they were the losers in the debates and ordered his retainers to shave the heads of seventeen prominent Daoists and compel them to convert to Buddhism. The Buddhist temples occupied by the Daoists and the property they confiscated were to be restored to their rightful owners. These penalties were relatively mild; Khubilai did not proscribe Daoism, nor were any Daoists imprisoned or executed.

Once Khubilai had dealt with the Buddhist-Daoist dispute, he received an assignment to assist in the conquest of the rest of China. His brother Möngke had devised a plan to attack the Southern Song dynasty. He would deploy his forces along four fronts, preventing the Song from concentrating their armies in one location. The troops under Möngke's personal command would head south from his base in Northwestern China in order to capture the province of Sichuan and then march eastward. His brother Khubilai's forces would move south from his newly constructed town of Kaiping and cross the Yangzi River into Song territory. They would there rendezvous with a third army marching northward from the province of Yunnan. The fourth detachment would move eastward toward Xiangyang and at that location join Khubilai's army. Möngke intended to isolate the western and eastern sections of the Song, and hoped that a quick victory in the west would compel the Song to capitulate.

Möngke's own forces faced stiff resistance, but he continued to march into Song territories until his death on August 11, 1259.

Once again, a *khuriltai* of the Mongol nobility needed to select a new Khan of Khans, leading to a cessation of the campaign against China. Khubilai himself ended his attack on Song China and headed north to champion his drive for leadership.

Khubilai and his brother Arigh Böke struggled for the succession, and each received support from other Mongol khanates, an indication of the fracturing of the Mongol empire. Arigh Böke represented Mongols who wished to uphold the traditional Mongol ways and values. He and his allies were concerned about Khubilai's and Hülegü's increasing identification with the sedentary civilizations. Moreover, they were perturbed that Hülegü and Khubilai sought advice and assistance from the subject populations, spent most of their time outside Mongolia and resided either in Iran and China, and married women who had turned away from their ancestors' shamanism to Nestorianism and Buddhism.

In 1260, Khubilai and Arigh Böke each convened *khuriltais* and had themselves elected as Great Khan, setting the stage for civil war. Khubilai relied on China for success in this struggle and appealed to his Chinese subjects for assistance in reunifying China. His main strategy was to capitalize on the plentiful resources available in the sedentary world and to deny them to Arigh Böke. Based in Khara Khorum in the Mongolian steppes, Arigh Böke needed to import most of his provisions, prompting Khubilai to initiate a blockade over the territories from which his brother sought supplies.

After several significant defeats, Arigh Böke's options were limited, and in 1264 he surrendered. Khubilai reputedly treated his brother magnanimously, despite his underlings' calls to punish or execute him. However, Arigh Böke saved Khubilai from greater anguish by contracting an illness and dying early in 1266. His demise was convenient for Khubilai, and this very convenience has cast doubts on the circumstances of his death.

Khubilai governs China

Once he became the uncontested Great Khan, Khubilai began
to develop a hybrid administration, which would appeal to and
incorporate both Chinese and Mongol elements. He was unwilling
to turn over too much authority to his Chinese advisers nor was
he eager to adopt the whole administrative apparatus from those
of traditional Chinese dynasties. The most telling indication of
his eagerness to modify the Chinese system was his refusal to
reinstitute the civil service examinations. Restoring the exams
would limit him to Confucian Chinese officials, and he could
not afford to limit himself to a bureaucracy composed almost
exclusively of the Mongols' subjugated population.

He also deviated from traditional Chinese dynasties by dividing
the population into three and, later, four groups. The Mongols
occupied the most prominent positions, followed mostly by
Muslims and other foreigners who would be recruited for
important posts in government. The Chinese of the North and the
Chinese of the South constituted the lowest-ranking groups and
were excluded from some of the most important civil positions.
High military positions were even more difficult for the Chinese
to attain or to aspire to. Khubilai and other Mongols decidedly
discriminated against Chinese of the official class.

Khubilai adopted these policies principally because the Chinese
vastly outnumbered the Mongols in China. One source estimates
that the Chinese in the North amounted to about ten million, and
the Chinese in the South accounted for another sixty million while
the Mongol population did not exceed one million. The Mongols
needed to retain control of the leading positions in government
and the military if they were to survive and avoid being engulfed
by the Chinese.

Yet Khubilai wanted to establish an administrative structure that
the Chinese would find familiar. Thus he restored the traditional

body known as the Secretariat to take charge of civilian matters and established the Privy Council to supervise military matters. He also restored the six functional ministries that had implemented policy in China. These ministries oversaw the civilian officials, conducted censuses and collected taxes and tribute, managed court ceremonies and religions and dealt with foreign envoys, trained the military, enforced the laws and administered prisons, and maintained the infrastructure. Similarly, local administration resembled that of earlier Chinese dynasties, with China divided into provinces, circuits, and districts.

The principal difference between the Mongol and the Chinese dynasties was the greater emphasis on control. Fearing that officials, many of whom were Chinese, might be disloyal and corrupt, Khubilai delegated more power to a government body—known as the Censorate—than had any earlier Chinese dynasty. Censors, who could be crudely described as spies on the bureaucracy and the local elites, would periodically tour the country to ferret out financial abuses by the court, the military, or local government and would report directly to the Mongol emperor. However, the Mongols often allowed local Chinese elites considerable leeway to govern their regions as long as they paid taxes and performed the police, judicial, and military services required of them.

Khubilai and the Chinese economy

Having established their political system by the early 1260s, the Mongols now had to tackle major economic problems. The Mongol invasions of North China in the early thirteenth century had resulted in the destruction of some towns, the razing of residences and government and religious buildings, and the massacre of hundreds of thousands of inhabitants, with some Chinese sources, including several later historical accounts, citing a vastly inflated figure of a 50 percent decline in population. Numerous cities would have had to be abandoned if half the population had been killed. Despite such exaggerations, the loss of population in the North and ultimately in the South after its conquest in 1279 was debilitating. Chinese peasants were uncertain about the intentions of their Mongol rulers. Would these new overlords simply expropriate their land and convert it into pasture for their animals? Would they devise arbitrary and exorbitant taxes on the peasants? Before embarking on a planned and orderly economic and social program, Khubilai needed to relieve this misery. During his first years in power, he responded with tax exemptions and relief efforts, and he prohibited his officials and his army from making exploitative demands on the Chinese.

Even more significant, in 1262 he established an Office for the Stimulation of Agriculture. This was an indication of the value he placed on agriculture. His most lasting contribution was the founding of *she*, self-help organizations intended to stimulate agricultural production, introduce new technology, improve flood control and irrigation, provide assistance for orphans, widows, and the elderly, and conduct censuses.

Artisans were still another group he sought to protect. Like earlier Mongol khans, he recognized the need for craftsmen. Because they had few of their own artisans, the Mongols relied on foreigners, particularly Chinese, Iranians, or Central Asians, for such basic goods as pots, dishes, and textiles. Infrastructure projects such as the building of a capital city also demanded the services of highly skilled craftsmen. Khubilai thus offered substantial pay and food and clothing rations to artisans, and relieved them of the burden of forced labor.

Merchants also prospered during Khubilai's reign, becoming a significant factor in global interconnections and history. The Chinese dynasties had imposed numerous restrictions on merchants because Confucian Chinese scholar-officials disapproved of trade, asserting that merchants did not produce anything of value and simply exchanged goods, a parasitic pursuit.

Like his grandfather Chinggis, Khubilai elevated the status of merchants and issued more paper currency, offered loans for merchants engaged in long-distance trade, built roads and canals to facilitate travel, and established a postal station system, which merchants were permitted to use on their journeys. Such Mongol assistance led to considerable commerce across Eurasia, both by land and by sea, and, perhaps as important, led to technological, cultural, religious, and artistic interrelations among civilizations.

Indeed, unprecedented contact between East and West was one of the most important Mongol contributions. The *Pax Mongolica*, or Mongolian peace, facilitated the exchanges of people, ideas, and technologies. The various Eastern and Western civilizations, which were exposed to foreign techniques and views, chose and modified whatever they borrowed from others to suit their own needs. Iranians introduced chickpeas, carrots, eggplants, and pasta to China; they translated Iranian medical texts into Chinese while a Chinese agricultural text was translated into Iranian, and Chinese motifs and techniques in porcelain influenced Iranian pottery. The Mongols themselves prized craftsmen and experts, and moved them from one part of their domains to another to produce high-quality textiles using gold thread, blue-and-white porcelains, and gold artifacts.

Doctors were still another group who fared better under the Mongols than under the Chinese emperors. During earlier Chinese dynasties, doctors, many of whom had little training, were relegated to low social positions. The pragmatic Mongol rulers valued medicine and emphasized it as a suitable and attractive profession. Khubilai, who was himself afflicted with gout and other ailments, was a particularly strong supporter of the profession. In 1285, 1288, and 1290, he dispatched envoys to South India to seek not only precious goods but also skilled doctors. Throughout his reign, he invited Nestorian and Muslim physicians from Central Asia and Iran, as well as doctors from Korea, to his court. In 1262 he ordered that medical schools be founded in circuits throughout

China. Such strong support from the government induced a few sons of the Chinese elite to study medicine. Because young Chinese men had been blocked from taking the civil service examinations, which traditionally provided entrance into the bureaucracy, medical careers became more attractive. The founding of intellectually demanding medical schools, a dramatic increase in the publication of medical textbooks, and higher status for physicians motivated many Chinese to enter the previously lowly regarded profession.

Similarly, Khubilai and other Mongol khans esteemed astronomers for their practical advice about when to begin and end activities, and thus recruited Chinese and foreign experts, eventually founding an Office of Muslim Astronomy at the court. They invited the Iranian astronomer Jamal al-Din to bring diagrams of astronomical instruments from Iran to China and to assist in constructing them. Jamal al-Din also offered diagrams and calculations, which helped the Chinese scientist Guo Shoujing in devising a new and more accurate Chinese calendar. The Chinese generally preserved their theories of astronomy, but the Yuan court adopted and modified specific Iranian instruments. Similarly, exposure to Iran helped the Chinese to devise better maps, with color coding and grids.

Khubilai and legitimacy

These policies of Sino-Mongol cultural and scientific accommodation helped the Mongols and Khubilai in particular gain support and legitimacy as rulers of China, but Khubilai's claim to universal rule as Great Khan had been seriously eroded. Both the Golden Horde in Russia and the Mongol khan in Central Asia had supported Khubilai's brother in their struggle for power and thus would not accept his supremacy. The Mongol rulers of Iran and West Asia were his only reliable allies, but they were entangled in conflict with the Golden Horde, further dividing the Mongol world. Although West Asia was virtually autonomous, the

Mongol rulers in Iran acknowledged a symbolic status as vassals of the Great Khan. Such amicable relations translated into trade and, perhaps as important, cultural, religious, and artistic interchanges.

Khubilai's attempts to assert his legitimacy as ruler of China met with better results. In 1267 he began the construction of a capital city in the heart of the sedentary world, an important signal to his Chinese subjects. Khara Khorum had proved to be an inadequate location for a great empire because it simply did not have a hinterland that could readily supply the city's burgeoning population with food and other necessities. Khubilai ordered the building of Daidu (or Great Capital) near modern Beijing and recruited a multiethnic group of craftsmen and laborers to work on it. The location of the city, which was farther north than most Chinese capitals, attested to his desire to have a base to control his native land in the North while continuing to rule China. Its only drawback was the lack of sufficient grain for a large population, which Khubilai resolved by extending the Grand Canal from the more fertile South almost to Daidu.

He ensured that the city would be familiar to the Chinese in order to ingratiate himself with them. The layout of the city in symmetrical east–west and north–south axes, the eleven gates with three-story towers on each that permitted entrance, and the divisions between the Imperial City, the residence of the Imperial clan, the inner wall within which officials lived, and the outer wall where ordinary inhabitants resided were all Chinese in conception and architectural form. The buildings within the Imperial City, such as the hall for reception of foreign envoys and the khan's own quarters and those of his consorts and concubines, resembled those of a Chinese capital. Lakes, gardens, and bridges crisscrossed the Imperial City, still another feature of traditional Chinese capitals. Yet Mongol touches were also evident. Curtains and screens of ermine skins hung in Khubilai's sleeping quarters, a tangible reminder of the Mongols' hunting and pastoral lifestyle. Khubilai and his sons often lived in *gers*, or tents, adjacent to the palaces. When one of Khubilai's wives was in the last stages of pregnancy, she moved to a *ger* and gave birth there.

As Daidu became more of a Chinese-style city, Khubilai's original capital was converted to other uses. Shangdu became an outlet for continuance of the Mongol rituals. It would serve as a resort and a hunting park. By the time Marco Polo visited in the mid-1270s, Shangdu had become a hunting preserve (with, according to one source, five hundred birds of prey), a means by which Khubilai could retain his connections with nature and the traditional rustic activities of his Mongol heritage.

A drive for legitimacy in China shaped others of his early policies. He constructed temples for his ancestors and performed the ceremonies associated with Chinese ancestor worship. Following the advice of his Chinese advisers, he constructed a shrine to Confucius. Needing to cultivate his image as a Confucian emperor, he chose a Chinese name, "Yuan" or "origin," for his dynasty. He also restored the Confucian rituals of court music and dance, accepting the view that omission or inadequate performance of these ceremonies would lead to floods, earthquakes, droughts, and other natural catastrophes. An even more telling signal was his recruitment of a Confucian tutor to teach Jingim, his young son and designated successor.

Khubilai also sought legitimacy with his own people. Like his forebears, Khubilai recognized that he had to persist in territorial expansion in order to remain a credible Mongol khan. Given the sizable Mongol army and its even more numerous contingents of foreign recruits, he needed to keep his forces occupied. Moreover, he would not be accepted as ruler of China without defeating the Southern Song and becoming master of China south of the Yangzi River.

Yet he had to be concerned with his northern borders. In the North, his ancestors had been frustrated in efforts to pacify Korea, but Khubilai succeeded in persuading the Korean crown prince to submit. Later he sent one of his daughters in marriage to the Korean king, forming the first in a series of marital alliances with Korea. He was not as successful in Central Asia. The threat derived from his cousin Khaidu, a fellow member of the Mongol imperial line, a grandson of the Great Khan Ögödei, Because Central Asia was the crossroads in commerce linking China, India, West Asia, and Europe, instability in the region would subvert Khubilai's efforts at trade and intercultural contacts. The struggle between the two cousins wound up at a standstill, and Khubilai eventually acknowledged that he could not control Central Asia. Despite this failure, caravans continued to travel from West Asia, especially Iran, to China and vice versa, often circumventing territories where Khubilai and Khaidu fought. Relations across Asia thus persisted and laid the foundations for global interconnections.

Conquest of southern China

Khubilai's most important frontier was to the south. He needed to conquer the Southern Song dynasty to avoid a Chinese nativist movement to expel the Mongols from North China, but such an effort would be demanding. Mongol armies and cavalry had been successful primarily in northern climates and terrains, and were unaccustomed to the heat and the more forested lands in the South. Their horses could not readily adjust to the punishing high temperatures of the semitropical regions of South China, nor could they count on much grass for their animals because the Chinese planted crops on all available land. Mongol troops needed to develop a naval force, which was essential in crossing the Yangzi River to reach the Southern Song strongholds and to attack cities along China's southeastern coast. Sophisticated siege weapons and tactics were also required to overcome the resistance of some of the world's most populous cities.

Although it faced political and economic difficulties, the Southern Song was a formidable foe. With rich fertile lands and extensive trade networks both within China and abroad, the dynasty was prosperous and could command considerable resources in a struggle against the Mongols. However, the Song government was riddled with corruption; its landlords often evaded taxes, leading to revenue shortfalls for the dynasty; and the empress dowagers (mothers of the emperors) or court officials controlled the emperors, the last three of whom ascended to the throne as infants.

Control over Xiangyang and Fancheng, two cities on the Middle Yangzi basin, was crucial for attempts to cross the Yangzi River. Seizure of the two towns would offer the Mongols a base for assaults on the rest of the South. In 1268 the Mongols surrounded the cities, but they soon recognized that they required supremacy over the nearby Han River to block supplies sent by ship. Moreover, they would have to storm the walls to overcome the well-entrenched defenders, an effort that might entail heavy losses. They thus needed artillery support to avert huge casualties, and Khubilai recruited two skilled West Asian Muslim engineers to provide such support. The two men sent by the Mongol rulers of Iran built a catapult, which devastated the town. After five years of an intermittent struggle, Xiangyang submitted in 1273, and Fancheng succumbed shortly thereafter.

From 1273 on, Mongol forces moved inexorably forward. In 1275 they occupied the wealthy and commercially important town of Yangzhou. They then were prepared for an attack on the Song capital of Hangzhou, one of the greatest of the world's cities. The Song court was confused and chaotic, with a five-year-old emperor allegedly ruling, but his grandmother was the real wielder of power. Recognizing the weakness of the Song's forces, the empress dowager negotiated with the Mongols, and in January 1276 she submitted. Khubilai, seeking to gain favor with the southern Chinese, did not harm the imperial family. Meanwhile loyalist officials fled from Hangzhou and enthroned one of the emperor's half-brothers, an infant himself, as the new emperor. Mongol troops pursued the loyalists all along the coast. In May 1278 the young, somewhat sickly emperor, overwhelmed by the pressures and rugged life, died. The loyalists then enthroned the emperor's half-brother, still another child. However, they were no match for the pursuing Mongol forces. Recognizing that the Mongols were about to capture him and the emperor, the leading Chinese official picked up his young charge, dove into the water, and drowned. The last Song emperor had perished at sea, and the Song dynasty had at last fallen to the Mongols.

By 1279 Khubilai had destroyed the remnants of the Song dynasty. However, he now faced the more difficult task of gaining the allegiance of the people of South China. As soon as the Song fell, he sought to prevent his forces from alienating local people. He warned against expropriation of their property or any other kind of exploitation. His policies turned out to be effective because few insurrections are recorded. It is remarkable that he was able to institute Mongol rule, with as few difficulties as he had, over the land with the largest population in the world.

Il-Khanate: instability and ingenuity

Like Mongol governance in East Asia, Mongol rule in West Asia was full of paradoxes. The Mongol khans stabilized the region after ending the turmoil of the later Abbasid caliphate in Baghdad. Yet political infighting and succession struggles among the Mongol leaders led to considerable disruptions in the approximately eighty years of their dynasty.

Hülegü, Khubilai's brother and conqueror of the Abbasid caliphate, did not end his campaigns after his occupation of Baghdad; instead his forces advanced to Syria. His troops occupied Aleppo and Damascus, and were poised to campaign farther west, although Syria may not have had sufficient pasture for the Mongol horses. After these striking successes in challenging the Mamluks, the last remaining significant Islamic dynasty in the Middle East, he learned of the death of his brother, the Great Khan Möngke. He halted the campaign and began to travel back to his native land to join the *khuriltai*, which would elect the new Great Khan. A small and vulnerable Mongol detachment remained in Syria, awaiting Hülegü's return.

Like the death of Ögödei in 1241, which ended Mongol expansion into Europe, Möngke's death had far-reaching consequences. The Mamluks' leader saw a tactical advantage in attacking the relatively minor Mongol army that Hülegü had stationed in Syria before departing to the East. In February 1260, the Mamluk forces, under their great commander Baybars I, engaged and then defeated the Mongol troops in the area of Ayn Jalut, capturing and then beheading the Mongol commander. The battle was not a major clash of two powerful armies, but it proved to be significant because it subverted the Mongol forces' aura of invincibility, a psychological blow that undermined Mongol efforts to terrorize enemies into voluntary submission.

Hülegü himself halted in Iran on learning that his brothers Khubilai and Arigh Böke were at war over the position of Great Khanate. He assumed the title of Il-Khan (or "Subordinate Khan") to the Great Khan and established the Il-Khanate as a semi-autonomous segment of the Mongol domains, a political act sure to elicit hostility in the Mongol khanates in Russia and Central Asia. Ignoring the obvious discomfort of his Mongol neighbors and deciding to settle in West Asia, he confronted serious difficulties in ruling in Iran and the Middle Eastern areas the Mongols controlled. The Mongol invasions had reduced the population and damaged the cultivated land. Yet Hülegü and his successors required increased revenues to support military operations, in part because of conflicts with many of their neighbors, and they began to impose irregular and capricious levies on the population.

They maintained harmonious contacts with only one of their immediate neighbors, the Byzantine Empire. Hülegü's wife (and stepmother) Dokhuz Khatun was a staunch Nestorian Christian and sought good relations with the Christian world. Negotiations with the Byzantines led eventually to the dispatch of Emperor Michael VIII's illegitimate daughter Maria Palaiologina as an additional wife for Hülegü. By the time of her arrival, Hülegü had died; his son and successor then took her as his wife. Michael VIII was not necessarily an ally, as he proved when he sent another of his illegitimate daughters to Prince Noghai of the Golden Horde, the Il-Khan's enemies. The Il-Khans were often at war with neighbors other than with the Byzantines.

Their conflict with the Golden Horde centered initially on competing narratives. The Golden Horde claimed that Chinggis had granted the Western Regions of the Mongol Empire to his son Jochi. In this scenario, although Jochi had died before his father, his sons Batu (r. 1237–56) and Berke (r. 1257–66) had inherited these territories, which included at the very least modern Azerbaijan and Iran. Azerbaijan, with its lush grasslands and its strategic location along the trade routes, was especially appealing to the Golden Horde. The founding of the Il-Khanate naturally challenged their claims and set the stage for war, with Azerbaijan as a significant prize. By 1262 the Il-Khanate's and the Golden Horde's troops battled along their borders, subverting Mongol brotherhood and spelling the end of the Mongol Empire.

At the same time, Chaghadai's descendants in Central Asia opposed the Il-Khanate. The Chaghadai khanate feared the Il-Khanate's growing power and knew that Hülegü and his successors supported Khubilai in his struggle with them. Thus the Mongol Empire bifurcated into a union of the Chaghadai khanate and the Golden Horde in opposition to the Yuan dynasty in China and the Il-Khanate. Sporadic conflict between the Il-Khans and Central Asia persisted until Khubilai's cousin Khaidu's death in 1301. These divisions confirmed the view that the tremendous size of the Chinggisid empire would inevitably lead to dissension and splits.

The Il-Khans confronted not only political infighting among the Mongols but also continued struggles with the Mamluks, who appeared, on occasion, to collaborate with the Golden Horde. After his forces' defeat at Ayn Jalut, Hülegü was determined to avenge himself on the Mamluks and their new leader Baybars I. Border sparring, raids, skirmishes, and assassinations characterized his relations with the Mamluks. In 1262 he dispatched embassies to King Louis IX of France to propose an alliance against the Mamluks, but the envoys and their letters apparently did not reach their destinations. After his death, wars with the Mamluks erupted in 1281, 1299, 1303, and 1312. The Il-Khans could not overcome the Mamluks who had a strong esprit de corps and an ever increasing military force. By 1291 the Mamluks had overpowered the city of Acre, the last remaining Western Christian presence in the Middle East, which had been a stronghold since the earlier Crusades. They could thus portray themselves as "Defenders of Islam," which elicited support from the Muslim world.

The political infighting from Hülegü's death in 1265 until Ghazan Khan's accession in 1295 generated considerable instability in West Asia. Abakha, Hülegü's son (r. 1265–82), succeeded to his father's throne without incident and, like his father, sought to create a multireligious and multiethnic bureaucracy to rule a largely Muslim population. Thus he recruited Nestorians, Buddhists, and Jews as administrators. Abakha also selected Tabriz as the site for his capital, still another indication of his desire to rule his newly subjugated domains. Its abundant water supply and moderate climate made it an ideal locale for the Mongols and their animals. Perhaps as critical, the city was on the main east–west caravan routes, offering lucrative opportunities for merchants and for the Khanate.

Tegüder (r. 1282–84), Abakha's brother and successor, converted to Islam, assuming the name Ahmad when he became a Muslim. His conversion prompted fears that he would end the conflict and ally with the Mamluks. Thus Arghun (r. 1284–91), Abakha's son, rebelled, defeated, and executed Tegüder. After his death, the succeeding two Il-khans were murdered; only with the accession of Ghazan did some stability recur. These irregularities not only revealed the disunity that had plagued all the Mongol domains but also the damage imposed upon top officials. In the almost eighty years of Il-khanate rule, only one of the viziers or chief ministers died of natural causes; the rest were executed or assassinated, an alarming sign of the seemingly uncontrollable infighting in the Il-khanate.

The Il-khans needed allies to cope with threats from the Mamluks and the Golden Horde. Because the Yuan dynasty was too far away to assist them, they turned to the Europeans, who still wanted to regain the Holy Lands from the Muslims. The Il-khans and the European monarchs and popes exchanged embassies in order to collaborate against their common enemy but proved unable to forge an alliance. The most renowned emissary was Rabban Sauma, a Nestorian Christian who was born in Daidu and had traveled westward on a pilgrimage to the Holy Lands only to discover that he could not fulfill his dream because of Mamluk control over these territories. He decided to remain in West Asia and lived among a large Nestorian community. In 1287 Il-khan Arghun, perhaps assuming that Rabban Sauma's belief in Christianity would ensure a cordial reception in the West, sent him to propose still another joint military campaign with the Europeans against the Mamluks.

Rabban Sauma had audiences with the Byzantine Emperor in Constantinople, King Edward I of England in Bordeaux, King Philip IV (the Fair) of France in Paris, and Pope Nicholas IV in Rome, and Rabban believed that he had an entente for a Crusade against the Mamluks. However, he turned out to be overly optimistic. Edward I faced unrest in Wales while Philip IV confronted hostilities with the Holy Roman Empire and Aragon, together with unsettled relationships with the papacy and Edward

I, which led to a war with the king of England from 1294 to 1298. The Europeans also did not entirely trust the Mongols. Rabban Sauma, whose mission could have influenced the course of world history but did not, did write a valuable work about his journeys, which yields one of the few early Eastern conceptions of Europe.

The Il-khans persisted in maintaining excellent relations with the Yuan dynasty, a relationship that proved to be vital for global interchanges. The two segments of the Mongol domains traded with each other by sea and land. They exchanged silk, copper, and pearls among other goods, and they each dispatched official envoys to the other's court. Even more important, Iranians and Arabs reached China, and a few Chinese arrived in the Il-khanate. The ensuing cultural diffusion was striking. Chinese physicians arrived in the Il-khanate and treated several members of the Mongol court. Il-khanate ministers ordered the Iranian translation of a Chinese medical text. Some West Asians learned about the reputedly curative powers, mostly for gastrointestinal disturbances, of Chinese rhubarb (*dahuang* or "big yellow"), a plant destined to become a vital commodity in the seventeenth- to nineteenth-century Sino-Russian trade. Chinese seeds and plants, including rice, were introduced into West Asian agriculture and contributed to Iranian and Middle Eastern cuisine. Conversely, West Asian maps appear to have influenced Chinese and Korean conceptions of Eurasia. Yuan court officials recruited Muslim and Nestorian Christian doctors, and Khubilai established an Institute of Muslim Astronomy to secure Iranian and Muslim expertise. Yet Chinese and Iranian astronomy, medicine, and agronomy retained their own native identities and did not become replicas of the theories and practices of the other culture.

When Ghazan became Il-khan in 1295, he developed new policies that altered his commercial, cultural, and technological relations with the Yuan dynasty. Having converted to Islam, Ghazan assumed the title of "Sultan" and ordered that Arabic script be used on coinage, an important concession to his subjects. He maintained contact with the Mongol rulers of China, but his new titles indicated that he no longer perceived himself to be subordinate to the Great Khan. His destruction of some Nestorian churches and Buddhist monasteries and his growing dependence on Muslim bureaucrats charted a policy that differed from the Yuan's multiethnic and multireligious officialdom. On the other hand, his conversion to Islam did not end the conflict with the Mamluks, his co-religionists. Each side presented itself as the true defender of Islam, and the Mamluks questioned Ghazan's true faith.

Because Rashid al-Din's history, the most important contemporary source, portrayed Ghazan in an extraordinarily positive light, a balanced assessment of his reign is difficult. Depicted as a reformer, Ghazan first instituted a campaign against corruption. Differing from traditional Mongols who favored nomadic pastoralism, he sought to support Iranian peasants by providing useful information on agriculture, by construction of irrigation works, and by devising reduced and regular taxes rather than the capricious and oppressive taxes levied in earlier reigns. He also attempted to promote trade by standardizing the coinage system and weights and measures. Whether these reforms were actually implemented is difficult to determine.

Ghazan was compelled to abandon an attempt to adopt the Chinese system of paper money, which would have required merchants to turn over their precious metals to the government in return for paper currency. Merchants, who believed that this policy was a transparent government effort to confiscate truly valuable gold and silver and thus give worthless paper to them, rebuffed the Il-khanate and actually forced the court to abandon this policy. The Il-khanate's lack of success attests to the power of Iranian merchants, who played a vital role in linking Europe to East Asia.

Although Rashid al-Din probably overstates the originality and impact of Ghazan's reforms, the sultan was no doubt an ardent supporter of Islam, including the Sufi orders. He built mosques, emphasized Islamic law and the Hajj, or pilgrimage to Mecca, and advocated the public reciting of the Koran. He also constructed an Islamic mausoleum for himself in a complex that housed two schools, a law center, a mosque, a hospital, a library, and a fountain and pool. According to Rashid al-Din's hagiographic account, Ghazan was well versed in astronomy, medicine, and natural history. However, he achieved lasting fame by commissioning Rashid al-Din to write a history of the Mongols, which grew in to the first attempt at global history.

Chapter 5
The Mongols and the world: part 2

Although the Golden Horde was the longest-lived of the Mongol khanates, few Mongols actually reached Russia. Mongol khans depended on their Turkic military forces and underlings to conquer Russia and administer the domain. Many of the Mongol invaders wound up in the southern Russian steppes and retained their pastoral nomadic society. Turkic commanders, Russian leaders, and the settled population were granted considerable freedom as long as they sent taxes and provided laborers for the Mongol khans. The relatively small footprint of the Mongols in the Golden Horde territories would appear to signify limited impact on Russia, but their influence, both deliberate and inadvertent, turned out to be significant. However, most Russians considered Mongol rule as the era of the Tatar yoke, a disastrous epoch in their history.

Russia under the Golden Horde

From 1237 to 1241 Mongol forces plundered and devastated cities in Russia, but the traditional Russian narrative of total destruction of these towns is exaggerated. The large number of wooden buildings in Russia led to great damage during the initial Mongol assaults and contributed to the image of the Mongols as destroyers who caused havoc. But by the time of their attack on Russia and eastern Europe, many Mongol leaders had recognized that indiscriminate razing of towns and cities was counterproductive. They began to realize that maintenance and reconstruction of these centers would generate significant revenues once trade and the rest of the economy had recovered from the initial assaults. Thus a balanced appraisal would acknowledge great destruction in some cities that resisted the Mongols but would also notice that other towns and cities did not suffer significant damage. Estimates of the numbers killed are generally unreliable.

Batu, Jochi's son and Chinggis Khan's grandson, was the supreme commander of the Russian campaign and was recognized as a great leader. However, Sübötei, a renowned general, was often in charge of the campaigns and led the forces in battle. Much of his success was based on the lack of unity in Russia, which consisted of various states and peoples without a central governing authority. The Mongols faced weaker small and independent principalities, which facilitated their conquests. Batu established a capital city in Sarai, not far from the mouth of the Volga River. He was determined to rule his new territories in the upper Volga lands, the territories west of the Ural Mountains, the eventual dividing line between Western Russia and Siberia, and the northern Caucasus, among other areas.

Once he settled in Sarai in 1245, he started to register the population in order to levy taxes and tribute, and to impose other obligations. However, it was an abbreviated and incomplete registration because he did not have a sufficient number of skilled administrators to devise an accurate and reliable system. Although most of his troops remained in the steppelands, outside the Russian centers, and did not impose themselves on their Russian subjects, Batu dispatched resident representatives (*basqaq*) to the important towns and cities to ensure the regular transmission of taxes to the Mongol leadership.

Nonetheless, two years elapsed before the relatively less experienced officials, facing considerable opposition from the Russian principalities, completed the registration. The census turned out to be more comprehensive than Batu's initial registration, and only the clergy received tax-exempt status. The Golden Horde could now levy appropriate taxes on agriculture, crafts, and commerce, recruit soldiers, and allocate corvée (forced labor) obligations, including the staffing of postal stations. Although the Golden Horde khans initially employed private tax collectors who sought to extract as much revenue as they could, they eventually determined that this policy antagonized the population. They then started to use government officials to collect taxes.

Berke, who succeeded his brother Batu as khan, shaped the Golden Horde's policies for many years. He had converted to Islam, one factor that led to wars with the Mongols in Iran. Territorial and economic disputes were more critical than differing religions in explaining Berke's conflict with the Il-khanate, but their differing religions cannot be discounted as a factor. They competed over Azerbaijan, and Berke resented the establishment of the Il-khan's presence in an area he considered part of the lands Chinggis Khan had granted to his father, Jochi. Thus he often allied himself with the Mamluks, his fellow Muslims, who had been in conflict with the Il-khans since 1259. His own successor also remained hostile to his Mongol cousins in Iran and the Middle East.

While the conflict with the Il-khanate persisted, the Golden Horde rulers in Russia started to promote commerce in their lands. Their capital in Sarai revealed their support for an urban economy, not merely the pastoral nomadic lifestyle to which they were accustomed. They accorded merchants greater respect than in earlier times and started to mint their own coins. The cities of Kaffa, based upon Genoese trade; Tana, based upon Venetian trade; Urgench; and eventually Moscow grew and prospered as well. By the early fourteenth century, about 140 towns had been established.

The policies the Golden Horde adopted resembled those of the Mongol domains in East Asia and the Middle East. By supporting commerce, they obtained silk, porcelain, and glass, among other goods, and exported their own manufactured products, including golden objects. Such commerce placed them in a Eurasian network, leading to trade with peoples in northern Europe, Poland, the Italian city-states, and southern Europe, and as far away as China. Like Mongol rulers elsewhere, the Golden Horde recruited native and Iranian craftsmen, and artisans catered to the tastes of the rulers. As a result, craftsmanship in gold and other metals, ceramics, jewelry, and tile work reached a high standard.

The Golden Horde also tolerated and assisted foreign religions. Batu's grandson Möngke Temür (r. 1267–80) recognized the Russian Orthodox Church and exempted its abbots and priests from taxation. Even with the conversion of numerous Mongols to Islam in the early fourteenth century, the government did not discriminate against the Church. Despite such Golden Horde support, the Church opposed Mongol rule.

By the early fourteenth century, the growing number of Muslims among the Golden Horde leaders and the similar conversions of Ghazan and other Il-khans laid the foundations for a brief period in which the conflict between the two Mongol domains ended. The Golden Horde khan Tokhta (r. 1291–1312) and Öljeitü, his counterpart in Iran, cemented a peaceful relationship, although they each claimed Azerbaijan as part of their own domains. The two rulers did not necessarily create a totally harmonious relationship, but the temporary cessation of hostilities benefited both. In the Golden Horde, it set the stage for the height of Mongol rule with the accession of Tokhta's nephew Özbeg (r. 1313–41). An ardent Muslim, Özbeg fostered trade, patronized the arts, and built new cities, resulting in prosperity for officials, merchants, and artisans. However, conflicts with the Il-khanate resumed during his reign, and commercial disputes with the Genoese marred the previously amicable relations.

Tumult in Central Asia

The khanate in Central Asia, which Chinggis Khan bequeathed to his son Chaghadai Khan, is the least well studied of the Mongol-ruled regions, and, in some ways the least stable and most contentious. Consisting of pastoral nomads and urban dwellers in oases, supported by a rudimentary agricultural economy, the region played a vital role in Silk Roads trade. Throughout the era of Mongol rule, more and more of the area's inhabitants converted to Islam. Chinggis had conquered the area, but Ögödei and Chaghadai sought to administer this domain. Ögödei appointed a Muslim named Mahmud Yalavach to restore the region's economy, which had been devastated during the Mongol invasions. Mahmud Yalavach fixed the irrigation networks along the Amu Darya and Syr Darya Rivers, which were the lifeblood of the Central Asian oases and towns. Once Samarkand, Bukhara, and other towns had been restored, trade along the Silk Roads, via Central Asia, could be regenerated. By the mid-1230s, with agriculture and commerce reviving, Mahmud Yalavach began to impose regular taxes and to provide a steady stream of revenues for the khanate. Despite his success, he aroused the Chaghadai Khan's enmity because he was Ögödei's representative. In 1239, Ögödei, reacting to his brother Chaghadai's objections, dismissed Mahmud Yalavach. Yet Ögödei then appointed Mahmud's son Masud Beg as his representative in Central Asia. The new appointee maintained a relatively low profile and served in a variety of positions until his death in 1289, continuing the valuable economic policies initiated by his father.

However, the same success did not characterize the Chaghadai khanate's other policies. By the 1270s, its leaders were at war on a number of fronts. Ögödei's grandson Khaidu persuaded the weak reigning khan to challenge Khubilai Khan over grazing and camping rights in modern Xinjiang, the border between the two khanates. A three-decades struggle persisted until Khaidu's death in 1301. Because Khubilai had the resources of China at his command, the wars did not devastate his dynasty. The Chaghadai khanate did not have the same resources and was indeed harmed by the wars.

The khanate was also bedeviled by internal conflicts among various claimants to the title of "Khan," including the descendants of Chaghadai and Khaidu. Nonetheless, by the 1320s, it compelled the Yuan dynasty to abandon parts of Xinjiang. But it had incurred extraordinary expenses in the campaigns. Simultaneously, it fought over territory with the Il-khans of West Asia, contributing to additional difficulties for itself. The almost continuous warfare harmed the agriculture that sustained the towns and the Silk Roads trade, which also relied upon the oases in the region. A series of weak and ineffective khans added to disarray in the Central Asian khanate. By the 1370s, the khanate was vulnerable, a vulnerability which the great conqueror Tamerlane capitalized on to conquer the region in the latter part of the fourteenth century, although he retained the khan as a figurehead.

The Mongols and Europe

Western Europeans, including the monarchs, the pope, and merchants, learned quickly about the Mongol invasions in Russia, Hungary, and Poland from 1237 to 1241 and were concerned about a possible strike against their own lands. In 1245, Pope Innocent IV convened the Council of Lyons to devise a unified European response. After discovering from Europeans in the Middle East that the invaders from the East would not harm official envoys, the assembled leaders dispatched several embassies to the Mongols. The pope sent two letters, via the Franciscan John of Plano Carpini, leader of one of the embassies, to implore the Mongols to refrain from attacking Christian lands and to convert to Christianity. John first reached the Golden Horde's capital in Sarai and then set forth on a long journey to the newly enthroned Great Khan Güyüg's court in Mongolia.

Güyüg, who was offended by the pope's missive, responded with a letter of his own, rejecting conversion to Christianity and demanding that the pope and the European monarchs submit. He wrote that "thou in person at the head of the kings, you must all together at once come to do homage to Us. . . . And if you do not accept God's command and act contrary to Our command We shall regard you as enemies." John's mission did not produce the desired results; the Mongols did not convert to Christianity nor did they pledge to make peace with the Europeans. However, the report he submitted to the Vatican more than compensated for the failure of his mission by providing information about the Mongols' military and culture. The pope and the European monarchs were interested in his accounts of Mongol tactics and weaponry, which he gleaned from his own observations and the reports of others, and later historians have appreciated his descriptions of Mongol customs, lifestyle, and rituals. His condescending report revealed that the Mongols did not use tablecloths or napkins and did not wash their dishes, which he found uncouth and barbaric. He wrote that his Mongol hosts were quick to execute their own people or foreigners who poured out or wasted milk or food, or who killed young birds.

European monarchs and leaders, some of whom, like the earlier Crusaders, were eager to recapture the Holy Lands, continued to exchange embassies with the Mongols in Russia and Iran in the late 1240s and early 1250s, and the Franciscan William of Rubruck was the most prominent European to reach the Mongol court. With support from King Louis IX of France, William arrived in the Mongol capital, but he scarcely secured a pledge from the Mongols not to persist in their military campaigns. Indeed his conversations with Möngke were not entirely amiable. He even debated clerics representing other religions in Möngke's court and was the first European to write extensively and derisively about the Nestorians among the Mongols.

Portraying these "heretical" Christians as ignorant and unduly influential over Mongol policies, he accused them of prescribing and dispensing probably harmful potions to the khan and his court. The account he brought back to Europe and offered to King Louis provided valuable information about Mongol food, religions (including shamanism and Buddhism), and clothing. He described, in some detail, the process of making *comos* (in Mongolian *airagh*) and expressed his disgust with the enormous quantities of liquor the Mongols consumed. Yet he was impressed with Mongol women who drove the wagons, milked the yaks, made shoes and clothing, cared for the animals, and produced felt. Similarly, he commented positively on the beautiful objects at the court, including the khan's elaborate throne overlaid with gold.

Hülegü's invasions of 1256 to 1259 and his occupation of West Asia meant that the Mongols needed only to cross the Mediterranean Sea to reach Europe. The Mamluk defeat of the small force that Hülegü left behind in Ayn Jalut when he traveled eastward to participate in the election of a new Great Khan persuaded him and later Il-khans that they needed allies in their struggle with the Mamluk rulers of Egypt. Exchanges back and forth between Hülegü's Il-khanate and the Crusader states in the Holy Lands and Syria did not lead to an alliance because the Europeans did not trust the invaders from the East. Images of the Mongols as anti-Christ and as barbarians caused them to reject any entente against the Mamluks. Yet the Il-khans, particularly Hülegü's son Abakha, turned to Europe, dispatching several embassies to propose a concerted attack against their common Islamic enemy. His immediate successors persisted in the policy of seeking an alliance, but their efforts did not translate into a specific agreement.

Later Il-khanate missions met the same fate. The unenthusiastic response for an entente reflected, in part, the lack of European unity. Conflicts among the various European leaders subverted calls for a Crusade, which would cooperate with the Mongols in a sustained campaign against the Mamluks. The Holy Roman Empire's hostility toward the popes, a rebellion in Wales against King Edward I of England, and ongoing tensions between the

English monarch and King Philip IV all precluded joint alliances against the most important Muslim state in the region. Nor were European leaders persuaded of the Mongols' trustworthiness. Some believed that the Mongols would turn against them once the Mamluks had been defeated. After all, the Eastern invaders had earlier encroached upon Poland and Hungary and had invaded much of Russia. They seemed bent on continual conquests. What would prevent them from unleashing an assault on their erstwhile allies? The fear of betrayal caused Europeans to be cautious about any collaboration with the Mongols. Without such Mongol assistance, however, the Crusader European states in Palestine and Syria were vulnerable. In 1291 the Mamluks overwhelmed Acre, ending European control, though not presence, in the region.

The debacle at Acre did not exclude Europeans from the area and did not totally undermine European relations and contact with the Mongols. Europeans, including the Venetians and the Genoese, continued to trade with the Mongols, a commerce that had become important starting in the middle of the thirteenth century. By the 1260s, these European traders had reached all the way to China. Because contemporaries paid scant attention to merchants' activities, firsthand reports about commercial transactions— quantities, prices, and conditions—are scarce. But Francesco Balducci Pegolotti, a fourteenth-century Florentine merchant who never set foot in Asia, wrote a fine description of voyages from Europe to China, which provided information about commodity prices, the specific numbers of men and animals required for a caravan, and the distances between towns and oases. Marco Polo and other travelers reported that merchants could find silk, spices, cloth of gold (*nasij,*) furs, mercury, precious stones, and aromatics en route. Venetian and Genoese traders continued to trade with China until the middle of the fourteenth century, when the Il-khanate ended and the Yuan dynasty faced rebellions. Despite occasional conflicts, Genoese merchants continued to trade with Russia for furs, hides, and slaves until the early to mid-fifteenth century when the Golden Horde declined and the Black Death engulfed Europe.

Marco Polo was the most famous traveler and merchant to journey to China. Marco's father, Niccolo Polo, and his uncle, Maffeo Polo, had reached Khubilai Khan's court in the early 1260s. Before they returned home to Venice, Khubilai requested that they bring back oil from the Holy Sepulcher and one hundred learned Christians. Supposedly, they were to assist in converting his people to Christianity, although a likelier motivation is that he wanted these educated Christians to serve as officials in ruling China. Instead, in 1275 they returned with Marco, who, in fact, served the khan during the next sixteen years.

Marco's account of his adventures and observations, which he recounted while in a Genoese prison to a storyteller named Rusticello who transcribed it, is one of the most renowned books in world literature. His work spurred Samuel Taylor Coleridge to write the poem "Kubla Khan," which included a fantastic version of the khan's "pleasure dome" in Shangdu or what the poet called "Xanadu." Marco's descriptions of Shangdu, the use of coal for heating, paper money, the well-maintained roads, the military campaigns in Manchuria and Southeast Asia, and trade and merchants tally with those found in the Chinese histories. His awestruck portrait of Hangzhou, the world's most populated city, was especially noteworthy. Its canals, its spectacular location on the West Lake, and its restaurants offering the finest in Chinese cuisine captivated him. Although Marco inflated his own role at Khubilai's court and failed to mention such distinctive aspects of Chinese culture as the Chinese written language, tea, and bound feet in his account, he did indeed reach China.

The tangible and immediate impact of Marco's and other merchants' and clerics' trips to the Mongol world may have been limited, but the cumulative influence over a longer period of time was more substantial. Many Europeans initially did not believe Marco's descriptions of his voyages, but his account stimulated European adventurers and explorers to seek seaborne routes to East and South Asia. Indeed, Christopher Columbus had a copy

8. Khubilai Khan, portrayed with Western features, meets with Marco Polo's father and uncle in this European depiction. Like nearly all Europeans, the artist had never seen an East Asian.

of the text on his momentous journeys and believed that his ships were headed toward the East.

Because Europeans wanted to obtain East and South Asian products transmitted by the Mongols, they sought and eventually discovered a sea route to Asia. Even before this discovery and just as ships began to reach South and East Asia, Islamic states, which were even closer to Europe, had an artistic impact on the West. In the fifteenth and sixteenth centuries, Middle Eastern motifs and technology influenced Venetian glassware and painting. Both the Islamic world and Europeans cherished Chinese porcelain, which started to reach the Middle East during the Mongol era.

By the sixteenth century, the Topkapi Palace in Istanbul housed a collection of about twelve thousand Chinese porcelains. Simultaneously, European demand for Chinese porcelains grew, and the wealthy began to crave and decorate their houses with such export ware. European paintings confirm both the presence and the value accorded Chinese porcelains.

The interchanges between the Mongol world and the West may also have had a devastating effect on Europe. Some historians assert that the Mongols, who may have been exposed to the plague in Southwest China and Southeast Asia, may have transmitted it westward, leading to the Black Death in Europe. Evidence for this claim derives from a description of what appears to have been the plague in a Mongol encampment in Turkey. Commerce along the Silk Roads, the diseased rodents accompanying travelers, and the ensuing relations among civilizations, which the Mongols encouraged, may have contributed to the spread of the plague. Yet more specific textual accounts are needed to definitively link the Mongols to the plague and the Black Death.

Within three generations, the Mongols had engaged with the principal Eurasian civilizations. They had conquered China, Russia, Central Asia, and much of the Middle East, had failed to vanquish Japan, Java, and Egypt, and had established generally amicable relations with Europe. Granting *paizas* (or passports granting safe passage through the vast Mongol domains), made of silver, gold, or other metals, to foreign merchants, missionaries, and envoys, they facilitated travel and interactions among civilizations.

Chapter 6
The Mongols and arts and culture

The Mongol rulers not only promoted relations among civilizations, but also supported specific aspects of the cultures of the lands they conquered. They championed Tibetan Buddhism and the Sufi orders of Islam, and acted as patrons for Chinese painters and playwrights, Iranian historians, and Russian goldsmiths. To be sure, such support often accompanied a political agenda. The Mongol rulers rapidly recognized that the Chinese, Persians, Russians, and the other peoples they governed demonstrated great pride in their religions and cultures. Mongol patronage would offer a patina of legitimacy among their subjects. It could also win over clerics, artisans, and artists and could establish a link with earlier, native rulers. The khans and the Mongol elites also craved beautiful and luxurious products. Even in their relatively simple households in the steppes, they had appreciated adornments for themselves and for their horses, including Chinese silks and their own gold objects. Naturally, their destruction of Russian churches, mosques in Baghdad, and Chinese imperial tombs have not and cannot be ignored, but their contributions to art and culture have not generally received much attention.

Yuan renaissance in culture and arts

In his domain, Khubilai first made efforts to cement relations
with Muslims because he needed them to assist in administering
China. They had invaluable skills as tax collectors and financial
administrators, and Khubilai attempted to recruit Central Asian
and Persian Muslims by offering them special privileges, including
rule by their own leaders and judges. He provided funds for the
construction of mosques and even appointed Saiyid Ajall Shams
al-Din, a Muslim from Central Asia, as the governor of the newly
conquered province of Yunnan. Muslim merchants, whom he needed
to maintain trade along the Silk Roads, physicians, astronomers, and
craftsmen flocked to China as a result of these favorable policies.

Khubilai was entranced by Buddhism, although he never practiced
any specific religion. A Chan (or, in Japanese, Zen) monk had
instructed him in the precepts of Buddhism, and Khubilai had
given his first son a Tibetan name, probably due to his contacts
with Tibetan Buddhists. He quickly recognized that Tibetan
Buddhism was the optimal form of the religion for the Mongols.
Its emphasis on magic and esoteric transmission of its message
and, most important, its approval of political involvement could
provide justification for his accession to power. Khubilai had also
invited 'Phags-pa Lama, a Tibetan Buddhist, to join his court and
instruct his wife Chabi. In 1260 he appointed the Tibetan cleric
to a new position as State Preceptor, or teacher, and early the
following year he named 'Phags-pa as the head of the Buddhist
clergy. 'Phags-pa recompensed his benefactor by proclaiming him
to be a reincarnation of Manjusri, the Boddhisattva of Wisdom,
and offering him the title of *Chakravartin,* or "Universal King," a
post vital for Khubilai's standing with Buddhists. Later 'Phags-pa
proposed the initiation of court rituals associated with Buddhism,
and Khubilai himself sought to win over Buddhists by not only
providing them with tax-exempt status and donating substantial
sums for the construction of monasteries and temples but also the
production of ritual objects and sculptures.

The Mongols had always prized the works of good craftsmen. Their appreciation of beautiful and useful objects provided Khubilai with the opportunity he needed to support the arts in China. Yet he had to sponsor cultural projects that transcended any specific land within the Mongol-governed territories. Too close an identification with Chinese culture could be as damaging as overly enthusiastic promotion of his Mongol heritage.

His approach toward the official written language to be used in his empire revealed his effort to portray himself as a universal ruler of a multicultural and multilinguistic domain. He recognized that a serviceable written language was essential for the operations of a great civilization. His grandfather Chinggis Khan had commissioned the development of a Mongol written language based on the Uyghur script. However, Khubilai, with his aspirations for universal rule, needed a script that could also be used to transcribe Chinese, among other languages, and to represent the Chinese sounds of the names, titles, and offices in China. The Uyghur script was simply unsuitable for the accurate transcription of Chinese. Moreover, Khubilai planned to use the official script to help unify his realm and sought to employ it to transcribe diverse languages.

He commissioned the 'Phags-pa Lama to develop a new script, which the Tibetan cleric presented to the court in 1269. Delighted with this alphabet, which was, in truth, ideally suited to transcribe numerous languages in his domain, Khubilai ordered that it be used in court documents and as the main written language in his empire, referring to it as the "State Script." Despite his efforts and his repeated admonitions, the 'Phags-pa alphabet never replaced the Uyghur script or the Chinese characters. It proved to be difficult to induce the Chinese or the Mongols, for that matter, to use the script. Thus most of the surviving 'Phags-pa writings are inscriptions on *paizas* or passports, paper money, seals, and porcelains.

The Mongols and Khubilai were also ardent patrons of Chinese drama. Theater blossomed during this time, with the growth of cities in the Song and Yuan dynasties providing a propitious environment for a golden age of drama. Theatrical troupes mounted performances consisting of singing, dancing, pantomime, and acrobatics, which appealed to a mass audience, including the Mongols. Khubilai himself invited several of these troupes to perform at court and provided support for some

9. This passport, made of iron with silver inlay, permitted unhindered travel throughout the Mongol domains. It was written in the new script developed by the Tibetan monk 'Phags-pa.

playwrights. However, he and his Mongol underlings ought not to be credited with the development and successes of Yuan theater. The Chinese playwrights were responsible for their own artistic creations. Yet the Mongols offered financial assistance to theatrical productions, and Khubilai built stages in the imperial palace compound.

The Mongols also offered considerable support to Chinese painters. Some painters, especially in South China, resolutely refused any collaboration with their Mongol overlords and became recluses, and a few turned to the acceptable Confucian outlet of painting. A few, such as the revered Zheng Sixiao, employed symbols in their painting as a means of indirectly criticizing the Mongols. Some painters and calligraphers received Mongol patronage, though, and had the leisure time to produce splendid works. Khubilai appointed Zhao Mengfu, the greatest Yuan painter, to a position in the Ministry of War and chose Li Kan, a renowned painter of bamboo, to be Minister of Personnel. Both were permitted considerable free time to paint and to produce fine calligraphy. The reign of the Renzong emperor (1312–20) witnessed the height of court patronage and the commissioning of imperial portraits.

Another Mongol influence on painting was in the choice of subjects. Animals, in particular, often served as motifs in paintings. It is no accident that one of Zhao Mengfu's most famous works is the *Sheep and Goat* (now in the Freer Gallery of Art in Washington, D.C.). Zhou sought, in part, to appeal to his patrons, and his numerous depictions of horses gained him devotees among the Mongol elite. Zhao's son Zhao Yong and grandson Zhao Lin, who both served as government officials, followed their brilliant forebear into careers or sidelines as painters and used horses as symbols of good governance.

Greater opportunities for women also played a role in Chinese painting. When the Mongols occupied China, a few elite women artists capitalized on the conquerors' more liberal attitudes toward women to come to the fore with their work. Guan Daosheng, Zhao Mengfu's wife, was the best loved of these painters, and thirty-three works attributed to her have been preserved in such major collections as the Osaka Municipal Museum, the Yale University Art Gallery, the Metropolitan Museum of Art, and the Museum of Fine Arts in Boston. Her exquisite and detailed paintings of birds and flowers appealed to the Mongol khans who often idealized nature and the countryside. Sengge Ragi, one of Khubilai Khan's great granddaughters, was an ardent admirer of Chinese painting and contributed quite a number of art works to the Imperial Palace collections.

The Mongols prized and supported the Chinese porcelain industry, partly because it was a source of revenue. Mongol officials acted as superintendents of the blue-and-white porcelain center at Jingdezhen, and acted as intermediaries between Chinese potters and their West Asian consumers. Both Chinese and Middle Easterners offered markets for these ceramics. The Mongols ensured that the porcelains exported to West Asia catered to the Middle Eastern clientele, as they alerted Chinese potters to West Asian tastes, conveying information about the shapes and decorative motifs that would appeal to potential customers from these distant lands. They instructed the Chinese to produce massive plates because Middle Easterners characteristically placed their food on such large plates, from which each diner ladled his repast to his own bowl. Mongol managers in porcelain factories also described Middle Easterners' preference for elaborate depictions of plants, fish, animals, fruits, and even the quintessential Chinese motif of a dragon rather than unadorned plates and jars. As a result, the Topkapi collection in Istanbul has forty blue-and-white porcelains deriving from the fourteenth century, and the Ardebil Shrine in Iran houses thirty-two.

In addition, the Mongols contributed to the renaissance of Chinese textiles. Mongol khans compelled Central Asian communities of weavers to move to China and its borders to interact with Chinese weavers, leading to the production of the "cloth of gold" (*nasij*) textiles that the Mongols prized. Weavers catered to Mongols' taste and used gold thread to produce clothing, banners, Buddhist mandalas, and tent ornaments. The Mongols themselves took steps to foster the development of luxury textiles. More than half of the agencies they founded in the Ministry of Works supervised the production of textiles, and the foreign weavers introduced Central Asian and Islamic motifs into Chinese textiles. Both male and female weavers had numerous privileges and enjoyed a higher status than in any other previous dynasty. It is thus no accident that the Mongols influenced and contributed to the technical and aesthetic advances in textiles during this era.

The Mongols' major construction projects, such as the building of the cities of Shangdu and Daidu, also invigorated crafts. Khubilai recruited numerous foreign artisans, one of whom was Aniko, a talented Nepalese whom the 'Phags-pa Lama recommended to the Mongol emperor. Aniko constructed Buddhist and Daoist temples, a White Stupa in Daidu, and a variety of astronomical instruments. He also may have painted portraits of Khubilai and his wife Chabi.

In short, the Mongols had more than a passive role in the efflorescence of Yuan art. Because Mongols were consumers of some of the products, artists and craftsmen needed to cater to their tastes, which in turn influenced their motifs and subjects (such as horses). The Mongols' control over much of Asia and their movement of artisans from one region of their empire to another resulted in considerable diffusion of motifs and technologies. Aware of foreigners' tastes, they also provided guidance to craftsmen who wished to trade their objects with the outside world. The Yuan government offered tax exemptions and freedom from forced labor for artisans, and established numerous official agencies for the promotion of crafts. It offered official appointments for artists and craftsmen in order to support their work. And the Mongols preserved the objects that were produced—in part, through the Imperial Palace Collection.

Iranian arts and culture under the Mongols

Despite the threats from the Golden Horde and Chaghadai khanates, the Mamluks, and a sometimes restive Iranian population, the Il-Khan Hülegü was an ardent patron of cultural developments. Like his brother Khubilai, he recognized the importance of learning and especially provided support to a new astronomical observatory at Maragha. His court was receptive to Iranian poetry and art, leading to considerable cultural and artistic development.

Iranian art of the Il-khanate era displayed the impact of Mongol rule. The Mongols themselves were not the calligraphers and painters whose writings and images adorned the Iranian illustrated manuscripts, and nor were they the weavers who fashioned the Central Asian and Chinese textiles. All of these beautiful works were produced by the native inhabitants. However, the Mongols played significant roles in their creation, for they transmitted Chinese textiles and paintings and introduced West Asians to Chinese motifs. Such typical Chinese designs as the dragon and phoenix began to appear in Iranian tile work and in illustrated manuscripts.

The scenes portrayed in many of the manuscripts, including the *Shahnama (Book of Kings)*, the Iranian national epic; the *Jami al-tavarikh (Compendium of Chronicles)*, the world history written by Rashid al-Din; and natural histories all derived from Chinese landscape painting. The depictions of trees, so-called cloud collars, and mountains resemble Chinese depictions of nature. Decorative motifs on the ceramic star and cross tiles from the Il-khanate's summer palace, the Takht-i Sulaiman, reflect Chinese influence in the form, once again, of dragons and phoenixes, which reflect royal power and symbols.

Yet the tiles portray stories from the *Shahnama*, which thus links the Mongols to their Iranian subjects and was significant in bolstering Mongol legitimacy to rule in Iran. Several surviving Iranian ceramics imitate Chinese celadon ware and incorporate such Chinese motifs as lotuses and peonies, plants not indigenous to Iran. The horse trappings and belt ornaments produced by Iranian artisans surely catered to Mongol clients, and even brass candlesticks and incense burners, used in religious ceremonies, had images of Mongols. The frequent use of blue, which represents the Mongols' Eternal Sky, in tiles and illustrations reveals the conquerors' influence. In short, Il-khanate art reflects the globalization of the Mongol empire and simultaneously the Mongols' adoption of Chinese, pre-Islamic and Islamic Iranian, and Mongol symbols to legitimize themselves and to facilitate rule over a diverse population.

Rashid al-Din is doubtless the chief representative of this extraordinary Il-khanate culture. A Jewish apothecary's son, he became a physician. As a relatively young man, he converted to Islam. Recruited into government, he climbed up the bureaucratic ladder to become the vizier or Chief Minister. However, it was his extrapolitical activities that revealed remarkable talents and skills. Rashid al-Din had multiple interests and wrote essays on subjects ranging from theology to agriculture. His fascination with Chinese culture prompted him to support translations of a Chinese medical text into Persian and to learn about Chinese calligraphy and painting. However, the *Compendium of Chronicles* was his most notable enterprise. The Il-khan Ghazan, concerned that his Mongols subjects' distance from the center of Mongol culture had begun to erode their link with their heritage, had ordered Rashid al-Din to write a history of the Mongols. With the encouragement of a later Il-khan, Rashid al-Din expanded this assignment to include histories of the Turks, pre-Islamic Iran, the rise of Islam, the Jews, the Franks (that is, Europeans), the Indians, and the Chinese, as well as a section on geography. On completion of his manuscript, he provided funds to his charitable endowment to produce one copy in Iranian and one in Arabic every year, which helped to preserve various sections of his text. Commissioned illustrations of the manuscript complemented and enriched his text. No doubt he had failings, as some sources accuse him of nepotism and corruption. Yet his contributions to Iranian and global culture cannot be discounted.

Russian and Central Asian crafts

The original invasions of Russia devastated some cities and resulted in the collapse of such crafts as cloisonné work. Yet, like other parts of the Mongol domains, the Golden Horde rapidly showed its interest in a revival of crafts. The khans, princes, and merchants sought everyday utensils as well as elaborate clothing, headgear, and jewelry. Their desire for lustrous and sparkling objects, including everything from belts to goblets, mandated the use of gold and silver. Moreover, emblems and symbols on objects served to legitimize their rule while specific Mongol motifs, the Eternal Blue Sky and symbols of the universe, helped preserve Mongol traditions. As the economy revived and towns developed in the Golden Horde territories, the inhabitants built mosques, churches, public baths, houses, and markets. Some artisans, influenced by their Islamic faith, fashioned mosaics in yellow, red, and blue with Arabic calligraphy, glass windows, and tiles. Özbeg Khan, a convert to Islam, ordered construction of a palace that used blue tiles and mosaics, and had a wooden throne covered in silver and precious stones.

The pace of craft production accelerated with the development of towns. Artisans rapidly catered to the tastes of Mongols and their Turkic subordinates by creating elaborately decorated saddles and belts, leather pouches, bags, and baskets, and rings, bracelets, and earrings. They also fashioned ceramic cups, plates, and pitchers, as well as objects made of bone.

Again, like other parts of the Mongol domains, the Golden Horde profited from the travels of artisans and objects throughout

Eurasia. Craftsmen readily assimilated Chinese, Byzantine, Iranian, Arabic, and Central Asian motifs into their works. Potters painted lotuses, peonies, and fantastic and real animals—symbols that were quintessentially Chinese—on ceramics. Treasure troves of Chinese silk have been found along the Don and in the Northern Caucasus. Weavers borrowed a variety of Chinese, Iranian, and Central Asian motifs, attesting to the globalization and artistic diffusion of the Mongol era. The images of the cloud collar, the dragon chasing a fiery pearl, the peony, the goose, and the phoenix derived from China while the deer and does, the gazelle, the parrot, and the feline predators originated in Central Asia and Iranian arts.

The Chaghadai Khanate inherited a long-standing tradition of artisanship and a large group of talented craftsmen in Central Asia. These artisans were proficient in metal work and mural painting, but the Mongols prized especially their skills as weavers. Textiles were portable and could thus easily fit into the Mongol

10. Excellent renditions of architecture and dress in India and Tibet illustrate the section on geography in Rashid al-Din's great universal history. Illustrations of manuscripts, including Rashid al-Din's work and the Iranian national epic, the *Shahnamah* (*Book of Kings*), developed as one of the great arts during Mongol rule of Iran.

lifestyles of continuous mobility. Mongol rulers and patrons were therefore particularly solicitous of weavers and offered special benefits and a higher status. To improve the quality of the Chinese textiles and to introduce new motifs and forms, they moved weavers from Western Central Asia, modern Afghanistan, and eastern Iran to China or adjacent to the Chinese border. They also recognized that the Uyghurs residing in modern Xinjiang were excellent weavers and recruited them as well to fashion the textiles they coveted.

The Mongols' generally tolerant attitude toward foreign religions, their love of beautiful objects, and their patronage of playwrights, artists, and historians challenge the image conveyed of them in both East and West. Depictions of them as barbaric soldiers dedicated almost exclusively to conquest and pillaging require modification. Their murderous rampages and rampant destruction cannot be denied, but neither can their contributions to artistic and cultural advances in the lands they dominated for a century or more.

Chapter 7
Decline, fall, and legacy

Since his emergence on the historical stage, Khubilai Khan
had had one success after another. He had triumphed against
Dali in Yunnan, successfully presided over a Buddhist-Daoist
debate, defeated his brother Arigh Böke, devised governmental
institutions and a tax structure based on Chinese models, built
two capital cities, gained favor with numerous religious leaders,
encouraged the arts, and, perhaps most impressively, overwhelmed
Southern Song China, the area with the largest population of any
of the Mongol conquests. However, starting in 1281 with the death
of his favorite wife Chabi, he started to face serious problems. The
Mongols had dispossessed the Confucian scholar-elite, which had
governed China in the past, and was hostile to Mongol rule. The
four-class system instituted by the Mongols discriminated against
the Chinese, who were placed in the third and fourth class, and
resented such lowly positions.

Perhaps even more critical was the empire's finances. The
expenditures on the construction of Daidu, the extension of the
Grand Canal to supply the capital's inhabitants, the organization
of postal stations, and the numerous military campaigns were
enormous. Khubilai needed to raise revenue, and he chose a Central
Asian named Ahmad to be his finance minister. Ahmad recognized
that the more funds he raised, the greater his power, prestige, and
income. Thus his first step was to enroll taxable households that

had not been included in earlier tax lists. He increased the number of households in North China liable for taxation from 1,418,499 in 1261 to 1,967,898 in 1274. Imposing higher taxes on merchants, he also squeezed out additional income from the government monopolies on salt, iron, tea, liquor, gold, and silver.

Chinese officials and some Mongols despised Ahmad, accusing him of profiteering, cronyism, and embezzlement. When Khubilai's son Jingim joined the opposition, Ahmad's fate was sealed. On April 10, 1282, a cabal of Mongol and Chinese officials assassinated Ahmad and, perhaps by planting incriminating evidence in his house, persuaded the court that he had stolen state funds. Khubilai ordered his body exhumed, had carts run over it, and then had dogs attack the corpse.

But Khubilai still needed revenue, and he now turned to a Tibetan named Sangha, who faced the same difficulties that confronted Ahmad. He sought to increase taxes and was accused of corruption, favoring non-Chinese residents, and theft of state property. Chinese sources criticized Sangha in particular for sanctioning the pillaging of the Southern Song emperors' tombs. A Buddhist monk opened some of the tombs and stole jade, gold, and silver objects to pay for the construction of Buddhist temples. His underlings also desecrated the corpses of the Song imperial family, a more serious transgression. They exhumed the body of one of the last emperors, which was still well preserved, and hung it from a tree for three days. These abuses reflected badly on the Buddhist monk's patron, Sangha. Such misdeeds compelled Khubilai to arrest Sangha in March 1291 and to execute him a few months later. Despite Sangha's death, financial problems persisted.

Similarly, many of the Mongols' foreign expeditions in the 1280s failed. It became increasingly difficult to achieve stability as the Mongol court careened from one reckless foreign policy to another. The most renowned of these expeditions was directed at Japan. The Japanese shogun had rejected the Mongols' orders of submission, resulting in a failed and disastrous Mongol invasion in 1274. The Japanese, recognizing that the Mongols would return, erected stone walls stretching from Hakozaki to Hakata on the Japanese island of Kyushu, a project that took five years, to protect against an assault. In turn, the Mongols recruited Korean sailors and Chinese and Korean shipbuilders, and amassed a sizable military force. The Chinese sources report that the expedition consisted of 140,000 troops, which some scholars believe to be an exaggerated number. In June 1281, a flotilla of ships from North China sailed toward Kyushu, and a larger armada from Quanzhou in southern China departed later for a rendezvous at Hakata. For several weeks, the Japanese soldiers prevented the Mongols from breaching the defensive wall, and then, on August 15 and 16, a typhoon struck and sank many Mongol ships with their valuable supplies and reinforcements. The Mongol troops who had landed on Kyushu had to fend for themselves, and Japanese samurai forces surrounded and killed them.

The 1281 battle would have important implications for both sides. The Japanese asserted that the typhoon had been a "Divine Wind" or "Kamikaze," and believed that the gods protected their land and would not permit a conquest of the Japanese islands. The Mongols suffered a disastrous blow, for the expedition's failure shattered their mantle of invincibility in East Asia. The psychological edge of terror they held over their enemies was badly shaken.

The Mongols' campaigns in Southeast Asia also resulted in devastating reversals. They made the disastrous mistake of not taking into account the terrain and the environment into which they would venture. They failed to undertake the vaunted intelligence efforts for which they were famous. They apparently did not realize that their troops needed to hack their way through the forests to crush the resistance of many Southeast Asian groups. Moreover, because horses were unsuited to such terrain, their cavalry, perhaps their most important advantage in combat, scarcely played a role.

In a famous passage, Marco Polo describes the Mongol army's most significant success. As he notes, in an attack on the kingdom of Pagan in Burma, the Mongol commander faced a contingent of two thousand elephants in the battlefield. The Mongol horses panicked and would not advance against the elephants. The commander ordered his troops to dismount and tether their horses in the adjacent forest. He then instructed his archers to take aim at the elephants, who were totally unprotected. The wounded elephants panicked and retreated, in some cases trampling their own masters. Neither side emerged as a clear-cut victor.

The other Mongol campaigns met considerable resistance and did not fare well. Guerrilla warfare, heat, and disease often took their toll on the Mongol armies and caused them to withdraw. An attack on Annam (modern Vietnam) harmed both sides, leading the Annamese king to send an envoy to present tribute and pledge loyalty to Khubilai's court. Campaigns against Champa (modern South Vietnam) had the same ambiguous results. One positive outcome was the dispatch to Cambodia of an envoy named Zhou Daguan, who wrote the first account of Angkor and its massive, twelfth-century Hindu temples (which began to be used by Buddhists in the thirteenth century). Even more disastrous was a naval expedition against Java in 1292. After initial successes, guerrilla attacks, the duplicity of Javanese allies, and the tropical heat forced the Mongol troops to retreat to their ships and to return to China.

The 1280s also witnessed a major rebellion in Manchuria. In 1287, Nayan, a Nestorian Christian who descended from one of Chinggis Khan's half-brothers, challenged Khubilai's control over Manchuria, a threat that Khubilai considered to be serious enough that he himself led his troops in combat. Khubilai's forces emerged victorious and captured Nayan. Because Nayan was of royal blood, he had to be executed in a bloodless manner. He was wrapped up tightly in a carpet and was trampled to death by horses and carts.

The death of Chabi, Khubilai's favorite and most influential wife, in 1281 initiated a cycle of disappointments and failures. Crown Prince Jingim, who had received considerable training for governance of a multiethnic empire, died in 1285, almost a decade before his father. Khubilai turned more and more to drink and food for comfort, and court banquets became increasingly lavish. His health deteriorated, and his diet contributed to the onset of gout, among other ailments. The Chinese sources reveal that in his last years he was extremely depressed and relied more and more on one of his wives to rule the empire. On February 18, 1294, in his eightieth year, he died and was buried in an elaborate tomb.

Post-Khubilai decline

After Khubilai's death, the Yuan dynasty went into a slow but steady decline. To be sure, economic, dynastic, and military problems had plagued the last years of Khubilai's reign. However, the later emperors exacerbated these difficulties while also subverting Khubilai's accomplishments. Although they succeeded, in 1303, in negotiating a peace agreement with the Chaghadai Khanate and Ögödei's descendants, which ended a three-decade conflict along China's northwestern borders, political turbulence in other areas accelerated, leading to declines in foreign trade and in relations with Central Asia, West Asia, and Europe. The Yuan dynasty became increasingly isolated, and no longer benefited from the commerce and the cultural interchanges that had characterized the earlier Mongol era.

Struggles for succession to the imperial throne repeatedly generated disruptions. Potential emperors needed to be Chinggisids, but by the fourth or fifth generations, there were numerous descendants of the patriarch. Like the war between Khubilai and Arigh Böke, these struggles pitted the defenders of the traditional Mongol ways of life and values against Mongols, who respected and were attracted by the sedentary Chinese agricultural society and by Confucian civilization and its extraordinary culture.

After the death of Khubilai's grandson and successor Temür in 1306, assassinations of emperors and murders of claimants to the throne hobbled the court for the next thirty years. The struggles for succession, on occasion, led to purges, undermining and weakening Mongol rule in China. The emperors' extraordinarily short life spans added to the instability. Temür was an alcoholic who died at age forty-one. Excluding those who met untimely deaths, succeeding rulers lived to the ages of thirty-one, thirty-five, and twenty-eight. His descendants and successors scarcely compared to Khubilai's almost eighty-year life span and thirty-four-year reign, and the brevity of their rule contributed to chaotic conditions.

Court policies also fueled the instability bred by the violence afflicting the imperial family. The dynasty subsidized the lavish lifestyles of princes and officials, a significant imposition on the court's finances. Court officials increased administrative costs by appointing friends and supporters to an already bloated bureaucracy. Bribery, graft, and other forms of corruption accelerated in the fourteenth century. Powerful and wealthy individuals bribed government officials to secure special privileges and exemptions. Such evidence of graft alienated the Chinese population and lowered the esteem in which the court was held. A number of officials attempted to curb these excesses and deal with the dynasty's fiscal problems by limiting grants to princes and by increasing taxes and fees. However, princes and other officials evaded the new regulations and continued to receive oversized court grants. Several of the emperors paid scant attention to combating corruption and to bolstering the military, further weakening the dynasty. Perhaps the greatest failure was poor maintenance of public works, which resulted in more floods and droughts, although the unusually cold winters of the fourteenth century also contributed to natural catastrophes. Disease, including outbreaks of the plague, further undermined the Yuan dynasty. Less abominable conditions could have prolonged the dynasty's life, but its political and economic difficulties would have persisted and created conditions for decline and collapse.

Disunity, as evidenced in the succession struggles, was a critical factor in the dynasty's fall. Like the earliest Mongol confederations stretching back to Chinggis Khan's era, the Yuan rulers could not bring together the various Mongol and Chinese factions. Mongols in the steppelands and their cousins in China were often the principal enemies, although the Central Asian Muslims, the Tibetan Buddhists, and other foreigners contributed to these conflicts.

Reformers were repeatedly stymied. One frustrated reformer facetiously suggested the execution of those surnamed Li, Wang, Lin, and Zhou, which would have killed off much of the Chinese population. A few competent officials proposed more serious reforms to save the dynasty. The Renzong emperor (r. 1312–20), following the advice of one of his officials, reestablished the Chinese civil service examinations, but he did not mandate that they be the sole criterion for an official position. Toghto, a renowned and capable Mongol official, tried to restore the army to its earlier glory, to rein in local officials, and to generate a regular flow of revenues. However, he aroused considerable opposition from other officials; the last Yuan emperor, who scarcely devoted much attention to his official duties and was irritated by Toghto's growing fame, forced him out of his position.

Disastrous floods in the late 1340s were the last crushing blow. Numerous people died in the initial floods or succumbed to the ensuing epidemics. Millions lost their lands to the floods, and the government, riddled with corruption and mismanagement, could not cope with this disaster. Bandit gangs, millenarian religious sects, and ordinary peasants, reacting to the appalling economic conditions, official graft and bribery, and repression by both Mongol and Chinese officials, began to attack estates and government offices to obtain basic necessities. From simple banditry, some started to move toward rebellion. By the 1350s numerous Chinese groups challenged Yuan rule. Zhu Yuanzhang, a rebel leader who had spent his formative years in a Buddhist monastery, coerced the submission of other groups and then turned against the Mongol rulers. In 1368 his troops drove toward Daidu, forcing the last Yuan emperor to abandon the capital. However, Zhu did not crush the Mongols. They withdrew, returning to their ancestral homeland and, over the next three centuries, limiting their relations principally to the Chinese and other peoples in East Asia. Zhu and his successors would continue to fear a resurgence of Mongol power, a misguided view because the Mongols were unable to unite and pose a serious threat. The Mongols became increasingly isolated, and their relations with other Mongol-ruled areas in Asia withered away.

Dissolution of the Il-khanate

In Iran, events following Il-khan Ghazan's death in 1304, after a rule of only eight years, reversed his successes and ultimately resulted in disruptions, which led to the demise of Mongol rule within four decades. His brother Öljeitü (r. 1304–16), a Christian convert to Islam who had adopted the name Muhammad, constructed a new capital in Sultaniyya and an extraordinary mausoleum for himself with eight minarets and a blue-glazed and double-skinned dome (it still survives). Öljeitü patronized the Shi'a form of Islam and supported Rashid al-Din in his efforts to write a global history. His support for Islam naturally bolstered the Mongols' legitimacy with their Iranian subjects. Excellent commercial and diplomatic relations with regions to his west prompted him once again to try for an alliance with the European monarchs. First, Genoese merchants traded with the Il-khanate, and then Öljeitü negotiated a commercial agreement for Venetian trade. Second, the Byzantine emperor Andronicus II gave his daughter in marriage to Öljeitü in return for Il-khanate assistance against the Ottoman Turks who threatened Anatolia. Believing that such cooperation offered genuine opportunities for close collaboration, Öljeitü sent two embassies to the European monarchs and the pope to propose an alliance against the Mamluks. Like Rabban Sauma's mission, these embassies did not translate into an agreement.

Öljeitü's death at an early age and the accession of his son Abu Said (r. 1316–35) resulted in the dynasty's collapse. Assuming the throne at the age of ten, Abu Said was ill prepared to rule, and his reign proved to be chaotic. Ministers took advantage of the Il-khan's youth to advance their own interests. One official falsely accused Rashid al-Din, the greatest figure of the Il-khanate period, of poisoning Öljeitü, and he was executed in 1318. Before his death, Rashid al-Din was forced to witness the killing of one of his own sons. The government confiscated his charitable endowment (*waqf*), which consisted of mosques, a library, a hospital, an elementary school for orphans, and farmlands to support the inhabitants. As he grew into maturity, Abu Said himself tried to be a good leader, and in 1322, for example, succeeded in negotiating a peace treaty with the Mamluks. However, the resumption of war with the Golden Horde overshadowed the cessation of hostilities with the Mamluks. Peace appeared to be elusive during the Il-khanate. Domestic policies were also unstable. Chupan, a minister who relished power, dominated government during Abu Said's youth, but he himself was killed in 1327 during a campaign in Herat; Abu Said executed one of Chupan's sons, and another son had defected to the Mamluks, who eventually beheaded him.

Violence, struggles within the government, and inordinately high taxes characterized Abu Said's reign, and his inability to produce a male heir at his death at the age of about thirty led to the Il-khanate's downfall. The Il-khanate came to an inglorious end, and over the next three decades Mongol, Turkic, and Persian leaders set up petty states, each with relatively limited authority. The areas formerly ruled by the Il-khanate had no centralized administration until the rise of the Central Asian leader Tamerlane (or Temür [the lame]) in the late fourteenth century. The Il-khanate's fall diminished the steady flow of merchants, missionaries, adventurers, and craftsmen, although a few voyagers continued to travel along the Silk Roads until the mid-fifteenth century. Mongol rule in China and Iran withered away, subverting earlier interactions among Europe, West Asia, and China.

Collapse of the Golden Horde

Similar problems plagued the Golden Horde in the fourteenth century. Disunity in the Mongol elite flared up, leading, on occasion, to killings and assassinations. Even in 1299 Noghai, who dominated the government from the 1260s on, and Tokhta (r. 1290–1312), direct descendants of Chinggis Khan, fought a bitter war over leadership. Such succession struggles persisted, and a devastating conflict erupted in 1359, which further weakened the Mongols. From that year until 1380, some twenty-one different Khans occupied the throne, with one murder and assassination after another. Meanwhile native princes in northern Russia, supported by *boyars*, or aristocrats, arose and capitalized upon the dissension among the Mongols to collect taxes and to become increasingly more independent.

After defeating the principality of Tver in 1327, the Muscovite principality, in particular, became the center of the most powerful indigenous groups and began to challenge the rule of the central government. The battle of Kulikovo Pole in 1380 provided evidence of this challenge. Prince Dmitrii Ivanovich ("Donskoi") defeated government forces, although each side attracted adherents from the other side. The battle was not a clear-cut struggle between purely Mongol and purely Russian contingents. Some Mongols sided with the principalities while others remained loyal to the central authorities. Nonetheless, it symbolized the rise of regional powers and the threats to Golden Horde dominance. In 1382 Tokhtamish, a capable Golden Horde ruler, avenged himself, overwhelmed the Muscovites, and burned down the city.

Tamerlane, the conqueror of Central Asia and parts of West Asia, had been instrumental in placing Tokhtamish, a direct descendant of Chinggis Khan, in power. The two men cooperated for a time, but by 1385 had severed relations and by 1387 were at war. In 1391 Tamerlane roundly defeated his Chinggisid opponent and actually occupied and sacked Sarai. Undeterred, Tokhtamish continued to challenge Tamerlane, and in 1395 the Central Asian conqueror once and for all crushed his previous protégé, reaching Moscow and also allowing his troops to loot Sarai. Trade in the cities, including Sarai and Azov, diminished considerably. Tokhtamish lost his throne, and the Golden Horde began a long decline. The Orthodox Church, with a center in Moscow from 1322 on, also began to challenge the Mongols.

Tokhtamish's defeat revealed the Golden Horde's weakness, prompting regional leaders to break away. In 1438 Kazan established its own independent Khanate, and in 1441 Astrakhan and Crimea also founded khanates. The Golden Horde's authority became increasingly circumscribed, and its people identified less and less with the Mongols. It continued to retreat in the face of indigenous opposition and, to a certain extent, non-Russians and so-called Tartars (Tatars), most of whom were Turkic, supported the principalities. These struggles ought not to be portrayed as contests between colonists (that is, Russians) and non-colonizers (Mongols or other non-Russian peoples); there was considerable diversity, ethnic or otherwise, in each camp. In any event, in 1502 Mengli Girai of the Crimea crushed the Golden Horde, although the Mongol-ruled domain had been fragmenting for more than a century.

Until recent times, most Russian historians have emphasized the baneful effects of the Mongol invasions and rule. They stressed the Mongols' initial destruction of cities, which in some areas was indeed devastating. But the Mongols surely did not introduce violence; the city-states and the various confederations in Russia had earlier engaged in frequent conflicts. Some modern historians have blamed the Mongols for cutting Russia off from the West. The arrival of papal emissaries and Italian merchants in Sarai belie that assertion, as does the development of trade networks in the Baltic. The Golden Horde's conversion to Islam, as well as its toleration and support for the Orthodox Church, also served to maintain links with the Middle East and with the Christian world in Southeastern Europe. Thus Russia was not entirely divorced from the West. Finally, some scholars attribute the despotism of the later tsarist governments to Mongol influence, a view that recent studies have disputed. To be sure, the Mongols emphasized service to the state in the form of taxes, tribute, and forced labor, and recruitment into the military. Pre-Mongol Russia did not have the centralized administration that the Mongols introduced, and perhaps the population was freer of state control. Yet the Mongols' domination of Russians was limited, and in most cases they remained in the steppes, far away from the cities. They levied taxes and demanded services, but otherwise they rarely intruded. They set the foundation for the concept of unity and for the ensuing Muscovite state but not necessarily for the role of the tsar.

Other views of Golden Horde influence on Russia are less controversial. Mongol organization, weapons, strategy, and tactics provided models for the Russian states, which emerged in the sixteenth century. Their use of cavalry prompted the later states to adopt some of their tactics. The *boyar* class gained power and privileged positions, and would provide leadership in post-Mongol Russia. Although the initial Mongol assaults caused great damage, Russia suffered no long-term devastation. Agriculture recovered, but, more importantly, trade grew exponentially. Mongol support for commerce led to Russia's participation in the Eurasian trade networks. Russia traded with West Asia, Northern and Eastern Europe, Central Asia, and China, and recent discoveries of Chinese porcelains and silks in Golden Horde sites attest to the wide scope of this commerce. Russia became part of Eurasia and its history.

Russia's own institutions were also affected by the period of the so-called Tatar yoke. The Mongols offered a tax-exempt status to the Orthodox Church, allowing it to accumulate considerable resources to construct churches and to produce beautiful religious artifacts, including icons. The church also profited from the tremendous scale of the Mongol domains to maintain contact with Christians in Western Europe and with the Byzantine Empire.

Similar Mongol support for crafts spurred production of exquisite gold objects, ceramics, and textiles.

The Mongol legacy

The Mongols' trajectory was truly remarkable. Within two generations, they transformed themselves from pastoral nomads who, on occasion, raided sedentary agricultural civilizations for booty and necessities into rulers of a far-flung and multiethnic domain. With the indispensable assistance of foreign subjects, they devised administrative institutions for governance and often fostered native religions and arts and crafts.

The collapse of their empire was, in part, due to their own internal dissension. A centralized administration proved to be impossible, partly because of the empire's size and the attendant transport and communications difficulties, but even more because of the conflicts among the four principal khanates of China, Russia, Central Asia, and West Asia. The lack of a regular, orderly system for succession to the Great Khanate resulted in devastating struggles for power, often weakening the victors. The Mongols were also accustomed to traveling from one pasture to another in relatively small groups. Development of an effective confederation of a much larger population did not overcome ancient splits among them. Struggles between those who espoused the traditional values of steppe existence and those who assimilated into the sedentary civilizations further accentuated these divisions.

The Mongols' policies also provoked the populace they sought to rule. The influence of the military in societies such as China, where civilian officials dominated, created ill feelings. Their military campaigns and public works projects necessitated repeated imposition of taxes on increasingly restive subject populations, especially in Iran and China. Income shortfalls arose as the native inhabitants either evaded taxes or could no longer afford the continual impositions. In addition, some of the expansionist campaigns in Japan, Java, and Mamluk

Egypt were ill-planned and costly, contributing to more revenue problems. No doubt as colonizers, the Mongols aroused considerable enmity, and their religious policies generated hostility. Although they professed to and often adopted policies of religious toleration, on occasion they turned against specific religions. The Il-Khan Ghazan initiated attacks against Buddhism and Nestorianism, and Khubilai Khan imposed strict limitations on Daoism.

It would be inaccurate to deny the appalling loss of life and the razing of towns and cities that the Mongol invasions engendered. They introduced a level of violence that had scarcely been seen. Even if contemporary sources exaggerated some of the purported devastation and killings, there is abundant evidence of considerable murderous rampages.

Beyond the destruction and violence, what were the legacies of Mongol rule? Not surprisingly, in every one of their domains, the Mongols affected weaponry, strategy, tactics, and military organization. The so-called *Pax Mongolica* also brought about the first direct relations between Europe and East Asia, leading to acceleration in the pace of Eurasian travel and technological, artistic, and religious diffusion. Iranian astronomy and medicine somewhat influenced China while Chinese arts and agricultural knowledge had an impact on Iran. Chinese silks and porcelains attracted Europeans, and Russia and Iran also became prime markets for a variety of Chinese products. To be sure, the Umayyad caliphate (661–750) based in Damascus, and the Abbasid caliphate (751–1258), based in Baghdad, had traded with the Tang dynasty (618–907) of China, mostly by land, and with the Chinese Song dynasty (960–1279), mostly by sea, but the number of voyagers, as judged by travel accounts, was far fewer than in the Mongol era. In addition, China was exposed to Christianity. Europe learned, via Marco Polo's work, about Buddhism and Confucianism, and Iran. Yet each civilization adopted only the foreign artifacts, ideas, or technologies that suited it. Moreover, each adapted or often altered such borrowings to fit its own needs and its own society.

The major civilizations that the Mongols conquered and then ruled generally remained true to their essences, albeit with some variations and additions, after the invaders departed. The Ming dynasty (1368–1644) of China, which replaced the Mongols, restored Confucianism and the civil service examinations, but it employed Mongols in its security and police forces, spied upon and imposed greater control over officials, established a Bureau of Muslim Astronomy, showed interest in Tibetan Buddhism, and produced more accurate maps and geographical works, all of which reflected Mongol influence. Iran and West Asia remained adherents of Islam, especially Sufism and Shi'ism, but Nestorianism and other Christian sects survived as minorities. The Muscovite state that emerged after the end of Mongol rule revealed scant Mongol cultural influence. Orthodox Christianity was the dominant religion, although the Turkic people who accompanied the Mongols in their invasions and settled in the south were principally Muslims. Central Asia, which had served as a homeland for Buddhists, became increasingly Islamic.

The political impact of Mongol rule varied in each region. The Ming dynasty allocated greater authority and power to the Chinese emperor and state in order to avert another Mongol invasion. Unaware that the Mongols had split into different groups and could only raid but not invade China, the Ming court became increasingly despotic. In this case, the Mongols inadvertently influenced China, and their continued presence along China's borders shaped court perceptions.

The Mongols' political impact on Russia has been difficult to gauge. They have been castigated for serving as the model for the tsarist despotism. Yet the Mongols had been declining much before the establishment of the tsardom, undermining the view of a specific Mongol influence on the new political institution. The Mongols' political impact on Iran is complicated to ascertain because Tamerlane, a Turkic descendant of the Mongols, and his line of Timurids ruled the country for more than a century.

The ensuing Safavid dynasty (1501–1736), a native dynasty that championed the Shi'a form of Islam, still had a large pastoral population, probably reflecting both the Mongol and Timurid influence. However, Safavid political institutions differed from those of the Mongol empire.

Perhaps the Mongols' most lasting legacy was sustained East–West interrelationships. From Mongol times on, events in Europe would have an impact on the Middle East and East Asia, and Asian styles in art, dress, and religion would influence the West. The Mongol invasions ushered in global interconnections and global history. The fact that the Mongols are mentioned in contemporary sources in Chinese, Japanese, Uyghur, Tibetan, Old Russian, Georgian, Armenian, Persian, Arabic, Syriac, and Latin attests to their impact on much of the Eurasian world.

Further reading

Allsen, Thomas. *Culture and Conquest in Mongol Eurasia.* Cambridge: Cambridge University Press, 2001.

Amitai, Reuven. *The Mongols in the Islamic Lands.* Burlington: Ashgate, 2007.

Atwood, Christopher. *Encyclopedia of Mongolia and the Mongol Empire.* New York: Facts on File, 2004.

Boyle, John, ed. *The Cambridge History of Iran.* Vol. 5, *The Saljuq and Mongol Periods.* Cambridge: Cambridge University Press, 1968.

Brook, Timothy. *The Troubled Empire: China in the Yuan and Ming Dynasties.* Cambridge, MA: Harvard University Press, 2010.

Colvino, Italo. *Invisible Cities.* Translated by William Weaver. New York: Harcourt Brace Jovanovich, 1974.

DeBary, William Theodore, and Hok-lam Chan, eds. *Yuan Thought: Chinese Thought and Religion under the Mongols.* New York: Columbia University Press, 1982.

de Rachewiltz, Igor. *Papal Envoys to the Great Khans.* London: Faber & Faber, 1971.

de Rachewiltz, Igor, Hok-lam Chan, and Hsiao Ch'i-ch'ing, eds. *In the Service of the Khans: Eminent Personalities of the Early Mongol-Yüan Period (1200–1300).* Wiesbaden: Harrassowitz Verlag, 1993.

Di Cosmo, Nicola, Allen Frank, and Peter Golden, eds. *The Cambridge History of Inner Asia: The Chinggisid Age.* Cambridge: Cambridge University Press, 2009.

Dunn, Ross. *The Adventures of Ibn Battuta.* Berkeley: University of California Press, 1986.

Fitzhugh, William, Morris Rossabi, and William Honeychurch, eds. *Genghis Khan and the Mongol Empire*. Seattle: University of Washington Press, 2009.

Franke, Herbert, and Denis Twitchett, eds. *The Cambridge History of China*. Vol. 6, *Alien Regimes and Border States, 907–1368*. Cambridge: Cambridge University Press, 1994.

Gernet, Jacques. *Daily Life in China on the Eve of the Mongol Invasion, 1250–1276*. Translated by H. M. Wright. New York: Macmillan, 1962.

Halperin, Charles. *Russia and the Mongol Impact on Medieval Russian History: Golden Horde*. Bloomington: Indiana University Press, 1985.

Inoue, Yasushi. *Blue Wolf: A Novel on the Life of Chinggis Khan*. Translated by Joshua Fogel. New York: Columbia University Press, 2008.

Jackson, Peter. *Mission of Friar William of Rubruck*. London: Hakluyt, 1990.

Jackson, Peter. *Mongols and the West, 1221–1410*. Harlow: Pearson Longman, 2005.

Jagchid, Sechin, and Paul Hyer. *Mongolia's Culture and Society*. Boulder, CO: Westview Press, 1979.

Juvaini. *The History of the World Conqueror*. Translated by John Boyle. 2 vols. Manchester: Manchester University Press, 1958.

Komaroff, Linda, and Stefano Carboni, eds. *The Legacy of Genghis Khan: Courtly Art and Culture in Western Asia, 1256–1353*. New York: Metropolitan Museum of Art, 2002.

Lane, George. *Early Mongol Rule in Thirteenth-Century Iran: A Persian Renaissance*. New York: Routledge, 2003.

Langlois, John. ed. *China under Mongol Rule*. Princeton, NJ: Princeton University Press, 1981.

Lattimore, Owen. *Inner Asian Frontiers of China*. New York: American Geographical Society, 1940.

Lee, Sherman, and Wai-kam Ho. *Chinese Art under the Mongols: The Yuan Dynasty (1279–1368)*. Cleveland: Cleveland Museum of Art, 1968.

McCausland, Shane. *Zhao Mengfu: Calligraphy and Painting in Khubilai's China*. Hong Kong: Hong Kong University Press, 2011.

Morgan, David. *The Mongols*. 2nd ed. Oxford: Blackwell, 2007.

Moule, A. C., and Paul Pelliot, *Marco Polo: The Description of the World*. 2 vols. London: George Routledge & Sons, 1938.

Olschki, Leonardo. *Marco Polo's Asia*. Berkeley: University of California Press, 1960.

Ostrowski, Donald. *Muscovy and the Mongols*. Cambridge: Cambridge University Press, 1998.

Rashid al-Din. *The Successors of Genghis Khan*. Translated by John Boyle. New York: Columbia University Press, 1971.

Ratchnevsky, Paul. *Genghis Khan: His Life and Legacy*. Translated by Thomas Nivison Haining. 2nd ed. Oxford: Blackwell, 2006.

Rossabi, Morris, ed. *Eurasian Influences on Yuan China*. Singapore: National University of Singapore Press, 2012.

Rossabi, Morris. *Khubilai Khan: His Life and Times*. Berkeley: University of California Press, 1988.

Rossabi, Morris. *Voyager from Xanadu*. 2nd ed. Berkeley: University of California Press, 2010.

Secret History of the Mongols. Translated by Paul Kahn. San Francisco: North Point Press, 1984.

Smith, Paul, and Richard von Glahn, eds. *The Song-Yuan-Ming Transition in Chinese History*. Cambridge, MA: Harvard University Press, 2003.

Vernadsky, George. *The Mongols and Russia*. New Haven, CT: Yale University Press, 1953.

Watt, James, ed. *The World of Khubilai Khan: Chinese Art in the Yuan Dynasty*. New York: Metropolitan Museum of Art, 2010.

Websites

Asia for Educators, Columbia University. "The Mongols in World History." http://afe.easia.columbia.edu/mongols/. Faculty consultant: Morris Rossabi.

Asia Society. "Homeland Afghanistan," http://afghanistan.asiasociety.org/.

China Institute in America. "From Silk to Oil: Cross-cultural Connections along the Silk Road." http://www.chinainstitute.org/education/for-educators/curriculum-resources/curriculum-guides-units/.

Index

Index

Z